ALSO BY STEPHANIE AND WILLIAM LASKA

The DIRTY, LAZY, KETO® No Time to Cook Cookbook:
100 Easy Recipes Ready in Under 30 Minutes
by Stephanie Laska, MEd, and William Laska (Simon & Schuster, January 2021)

The DIRTY, LAZY, KETO® Dirt Cheap Cookbook:
100 Easy Recipes to Save Money & Time!
by Stephanie Laska, MEd, and William Laska (Simon & Schuster, 2020)

The DIRTY, LAZY, KETO® Cookbook: Bend the Rules to Lose the Weight!
by Stephanie Laska, MEd, and William Laska (Simon & Schuster, 2020)

DIRTY, LAZY, KETO®: Get Started Losing Weight While Breaking the Rules
by Stephanie Laska (St. Martin's Essentials, 2020)

DIRTY, LAZY, KETO® Fast Food Guide: 10 Carbs or Less
by William Laska and Stephanie Laska, MEd (2018)

THE DIRTY, LAZY, KETO 5-INGREDIENT COOKBOOK

100 Easy-Peasy Recipes Low in Carbs, Big on Flavor

THE DIRTY, LAZY, KETO

100 Easy-Peasy Recipes Low in Carbs, Big on Flavor

5-INGREDIENT COOKBOOK

Stephanie Laska, MEd, and William Laska

ADAMS MEDIA

New York   London   Toronto   Sydney   New Delhi

Adams Media
An Imprint of Simon & Schuster, Inc.
100 Technology Center Drive
Stoughton, Massachusetts 02072

First Adams Media trade paperback edition June 2021

ADAMS MEDIA and colophon are trademarks of Simon & Schuster.

For information about special discounts for bulk purchases, please contact Simon & Schuster Special Sales at 1-866-506-1949 or business@simonandschuster.com.

The Simon & Schuster Speakers Bureau can bring authors to your live event. For more information or to book an event contact the Simon & Schuster Speakers Bureau at 1-866-248-3049 or visit our website at www.simonspeakers.com.

Interior design by Colleen Cunningham
Interior photographs by James Stefiuk
Interior images © Getty Images/maglyvi, nadyaillyustrator, Serhii Sereda, Nadzeya_Dzivakova, petite_lili, LanaMay; 123RF/sudowoodo, macrovector, Aksana Chubis, Mikalai Manyshau
Author photos by Charlotte Laska

Manufactured in the United States of America

4 2023

Library of Congress Cataloging-in-Publication Data
Names: Laska, Stephanie, author. | Laska, William, author.
Title: The DIRTY, LAZY, KETO® 5-ingredient cookbook / Stephanie Laska, MEd, and William Laska.
Description: First Adams Media trade paperback edition. | Stoughton, MA: Adams Media, 2021. | Series: DIRTY, LAZY, KETO | Includes index.
Identifiers: LCCN 2021000304 | ISBN 9781507216088 (pb) | ISBN 9781507216095 (ebook)
Subjects: LCSH: Ketogenic diet. | Reducing diets--Recipes. | Low-carbohydrate diet. | LCGFT: Cookbooks.
Classification: LCC RM237.73 .L368 2021 | DDC 641.5/6383--dc23
LC record available at https://lccn.loc.gov/2021000304

ISBN 978-1-5072-1608-8
ISBN 978-1-5072-1609-5 (ebook)

Always follow safety and commonsense cooking protocols while using kitchen utensils, operating ovens and stoves, and handling uncooked food. If children are assisting in the preparation of any recipe, they should always be supervised by an adult.

The information in this book should not be used for diagnosing or treating any health problem. Not all diet and exercise plans suit everyone. You should always consult a trained medical professional before starting a diet, taking any form of medication, or embarking on any fitness or weight training program. The author and publisher disclaim any liability arising directly or indirectly from the use of this book.

DEDICATION

The majority of this cookbook was written on a treadmill, *not* in the kitchen. My excessive taste-testing of DIRTY, LAZY, KETO recipes was starting to catch up with me on the backend (literally), so I decided to do something about it. Sure, it took some finessing (have you ever tried walking and typing simultaneously?) and a few near accidents (flying off the back!), but eventually, I got the hang of it. Now, working at my standing treadmill desk feels like second nature.

I'm no stranger to making excuses. I spent decades of my life convincing myself I was "too busy" or "too tired" to lose weight. I would fabricate long lists of reasons why I couldn't change my eating habits, from the ridiculous (I'm big boned) to the simply-not-true (I can't afford healthy food). Ironically, my excuses never made me feel any better. I still felt lost in the plus-size department without an exit plan.

When I discovered the DIRTY, LAZY, KETO way of eating, all of that changed. Overcoming stumbling blocks became much easier once I changed my perspective. I realized the only thing stopping me, well, *was me!*

Let's hold each other accountable. No more excuses. If you don't know how to meal prep or feel intimidated by the keto diet, I'm dedicating this book to you. I promise to streamline instructions and keep the recipes simple.

I'm here to help you, my friend. Let's do this together.

—Stephanie

To readers everywhere who are sick of the constant struggle to lose weight and stay healthy. This book is dedicated to you. Thank you for trusting in us and the DIRTY, LAZY, KETO way of eating. Keep an open mind and stick to the basics of this low-carb diet. The results will show themselves in no time.

To my wonderful children Charlotte and Alex. Thank you for your bottomless patience in hearing mom and dad talk endlessly about DIRTY, LAZY, KETO and its benefits. May your lives benefit from witnessing our tireless work and passion to help others.

—William

CONTENTS

To discover what these recipe icons mean, turn to page 19.

PREFACE

Weight loss shouldn't be so complicated. Many of us have been brainwashed to believe that sweeping life changes are required to lose weight. Join a gym, sign up for a boot camp, follow a thirty-day meal plan? *That's the answer!* But grand gestures only work in the movies. In reality? Most of us fizzle out before we even get started. The thought of running 26.2 miles, going to the gym every day, and cooking specialty meals forever…is *overwhelming*. We stop before we even start.

Losing weight doesn't have to take over your life. I learned this secret while losing 140 pounds (about half of my body weight). My strategy was simple. I focused on making good decisions, *tiny little decisions*, day in and day out. That's it. Does my answer surprise you? I'm talking about the snap decisions most of us make about food without giving it a second thought. When I find myself rationalizing "just this once" or "one bite doesn't count," I stop and think again. For me, these seemingly inconsequential decisions are what matter the most. Tiny decisions have a snowball effect. They add up fast! For me, **consistency** (not boot camp) **has been the secret to sustained weight loss**.

Tiny decisions about what we eat matter. It's that simple.

But making healthy choices only becomes easier—and enjoyable—*once you know what to eat.* My version of the keto diet, DIRTY, LAZY, KETO, is much easier to understand and follow compared to what you may have read about. It's *kinda sorta* similar to a traditional keto diet…but not the same! Yes, I eat foods that are higher in fat, moderate in protein, and lower in carbohydrates, but I do so in a less restrictive way. This is why DIRTY, LAZY, KETO is so doable! Let me explain.

I'm not obsessively picky about recording every morsel I eat, nor am I snobby about the ingredients I buy. I don't purchase organic produce or specialty keto ingredients. *Do I look like a Rockefeller?* I buy what's on sale at grocery stores and order off the dollar menu at fast food restaurants. I don't religiously weigh or measure my food (I've never been good at math!). I don't count calories—only net carbs. I use the very sophisticated "eyeball" method when calculating serving sizes. I'm not perfect by any means, *and that's okay with me!*

I'm in this for the long haul—convenience and cost matter to me more than following a bunch of arbitrary rules that govern keto. Call my way keto-*ish* or criticize my philosophy if you want to, but DIRTY, LAZY, KETO has helped hundreds of thousands of men and women *from around the world* lose weight. If that isn't evidence of success, I don't know what is!

"My husband and I each have lost almost 100 pounds…DLK has been the best thing that ever happened to our diet. We consider it to be a lifestyle change."—Michelle R.

"Losing weight, feeling good about myself again…more confidence than I have had in twenty years!"—Michelle S.

"The day after finishing the book, I started my lifestyle change…. I never looked back. Eighty-two pounds down since the beginning of January."—Theresa

"The idea of not having to be perfect has helped me to embrace keto eating!"—Jennifer

"My whole life I have been trying to find something that works for me (oh, the money I have spent). And for once, I am truly excited about losing weight on my own terms!"—Nettie

I want you to have the same weight loss success. I'll explain what foods to eat, but more importantly, in *The DIRTY, LAZY, KETO® 5-Ingredient Cookbook*, I'll explain *why*. Together, we'll set up your kitchen for success, quickly review keto cooking principles, and then jump right into making mouthwatering dishes. You'll finish knowing how to make one hundred keto-friendly recipes using only a handful of ingredients. That sounds doable, right? The plan is to make cooking your way to weight loss as simple as possible. The net carbs and nutrition information for each recipe are even calculated for you. *You can do this!*

By reviewing the basics and keeping recipes simple, we'll remove any potential obstacles currently in your way.

You don't have to be a professional chef or a mathematician to lose weight with DIRTY, LAZY, KETO. There are no fancy-pants ingredients required or complex ratios for you to figure out. My strategy is stripped down to the bare essentials. I promise to explain everything in simple, easy-to-understand terms. You won't need a calculator or a kitchen scale—just a willingness to consistently make good decisions, one after another.

You can achieve your weight loss goals. Let's get started!

INTRODUCTION

Losing weight with keto shouldn't be so complicated or require a boatload of ridiculous ingredients. I was able to lose 140 pounds and keep that weight off for eight years by creating my own rebellious version of the ketogenic diet, which I call DIRTY, LAZY, KETO. Meals are made from "normal people" foods, from "normal people" stores (often bought with a coupon). I believe in keeping the ingredient list as brief as possible. I can count the number of main ingredients I use on one hand!

In *The DIRTY, LAZY, KETO® 5-Ingredient Cookbook*, you'll find one hundred great-tasting, no-fuss recipes—all with 10 grams of net carbs or less—that require only an armful of everyday ingredients. Keeping your ingredients simple not only saves you money and aggravation, but also time. When you can make an entire keto meal from foods you already have on hand with no unnecessary trips to the store, you are *winning*, people!

Inside this book, you'll find delicious breakfast, snack, entrée, and dessert ideas that will appeal to the *entire* family. You'll also get the advice you need about what you should be eating, why you should be eating it, and how to set yourself up for weight loss success.

> It turns out a lot of those keto "rules" aren't really necessary, after all. My way works too!

I'll explain this whole enchilada in three steps:

1 **DLK basics**—why this works and how to get started.
2 **Keto cooking simplified**—quick overview of setting up your kitchen for success.
3 **Let's eat!**—one hundred trusted, home-cooked recipes made with five main ingredients or less.

In addition, every recipe includes Tips & Options to help you customize the flavors to match your family's tastes. I also designate how recipes meet a variety of needs by assigning these helpful recipe icons throughout the cookbook:

 No Cook: Mix, fix, and enjoy! *Ultra lazy.*

 Less Mess: One pot—one bowl? *Minimal* dish-washing.

 I'm Hangry! Big-eater meals to *fill you up!*

 Picky Eaters? *He likes it! She likes it!* Crowd-pleasing favorites.

 Fancy Enough for Guests: *Ooh la la…* Looks impressive and tastes great!

 Vegetarian-"ish": *"Kinda"* meatless, but may still call for dairy and/or eggs.

My DIRTY, LAZY, KETO method is a flexible, honest, real-world approach that is doable for everyone. The recipes you'll find in this book are stress-free and uncomplicated. Whether you're a keto beginner or a low-carb veteran looking for a streamlined approach, let me welcome you to an easier way to "do keto." *The DIRTY, LAZY, KETO 5-Ingredient Cookbook* will arm you with the skill set and encouragement needed to cook your way to weight loss. And if you can bear my sense of humor, I might even entertain you along the way!

DIRTY, LAZY, KETO

Secrets for Success

.

CHAPTER 1

AN EASIER WAY TO KETO

IMPERFECT KETO IS JUST PERFECT

I'd like you to lean in—really close. I want to let you in on a little secret. It turns out, **you don't have to be perfect at keto to lose weight**. It's true! Contrary to what other people might tell you, you don't have to be in ketosis all of the time. Rules are made to be broken, my friend, and I'm the most rebellious eater you'll ever meet.

I never "ate clean" twenty-four seven. I couldn't do complex math problems (about **macros** or anything else!) to save my life. Despite my shortcomings, "doing my best" worked out pretty well. I lost 140 pounds! At the time, I didn't understand what was happening *metabolically*; it turns out I didn't need to. Together, these facts led me to the following realization:

> You don't need to be a top-level nutrition expert in order to lose weight with the **ketogenic** way of eating.

Stop overthinking keto. Suppress the urge to learn "everything" before starting (which would be overwhelming!). Worse, that kind of thinking might paralyze you from taking action. I'm going to break it down and explain only what you *really* need to know. By focusing on big picture concepts, I'll quickly teach you why my twist on the popular ketosis diet is so darn effective. Hundreds of thousands of DIRTY, LAZY, KETO fans from all over the world have lost weight using my strategy. It works! You can do this too. Let's start from the top.

UNSOLVED MYSTERY—DLK WEIGHT LOSS

How does DIRTY, LAZY, KETO help people lose weight? The answer is twofold: It's both physical and psychological—it works from the inside and the outside. *Say what?*

1   Physically, when the body is fueled by foods that are higher in fat, moderate in protein, and lower in carbohydrates, it enters a state of **ketosis**, or fat-burning mode. *Score!*
2   Emotionally, eating **fat** is satisfying. It tastes good! You don't feel like you're on a "diet." Not feeling deprived is a key component of sustainable weight loss with DIRTY, LAZY, KETO.

Keto Without So Many Rules

With DIRTY, LAZY, KETO, you can continue to enjoy all of your favorite foods without guilt or judgment—the trick is to make them in a new and improved way. Let go of the FOMO. It's normal to crave sweets, hit a drive-thru, or take shortcuts in the kitchen. I want you to stop feeling guilty about these so-called "bad habits" and learn to modify them instead. There is always a DLK solution.

You might be wondering if DIRTY, LAZY, KETO foods are expensive. Let me assure you that's definitely not the case. Shop at stores where you feel comfortable. You don't have to buy organic, line-caught, or free-range ingredients—I never did. Spending more money on groceries won't help you lose weight any faster. Buy groceries within your family's budget and value system and let go of the guilt. I've always shopped at discount grocery stores. I plan meals around what's on sale. **Normal foods at "normal people" grocery stores are all you need**—nothing fancy is ever required.

Fat Is Fabulous

There are no "fat goals" for you to reach each day on DIRTY, LAZY, KETO. This differentiates my way of eating from the

Strict Keto diet. Instead, I recommend using fat to make healthy food taste better, like having butter on your vegetables, for example.

> With DIRTY, LAZY, KETO, you'll learn to build your meals with three components in mind: **protein** + vegetable + fat. *Done!*

Eating fat (combined with protein and low-carb vegetables) makes you feel fuller and more satisfied. This combination naturally curbs hunger, which results in less overeating and, over time, weight loss. Additionally, this strategy keeps your body in ketosis. Blood sugar levels stabilize when fueled by fat. Why does that matter? Fluctuating blood sugar levels lead to moodiness and a desire to eat carbs again *for a quick fix*. Eating foods high in carbs, though, causes the entire cycle to repeat itself. Ketosis prevents that from happening. Magical!

Use Common Sense

DIRTY, LAZY, KETO is not an all-you-can-eat buffet. Just because a food is higher in fat, moderate in protein, and lower in carbs, it does not mean you can consume it in excessive amounts or quantities. Don't unfriend me for telling you the truth. There are no hall passes or shortcuts when it comes to nutrition. Every morsel of food we eat counts. I lost 140 pounds by eating a range of 20–50 grams of net carbs per day, but I spent those carbs wisely. As I explain in the **DIRTY, LAZY, KETO Food Pyramid** later in this chapter, I recommend investing the majority of your daily net carbs with low-carb veggies, lean meats, and healthy fats, and closely monitoring (limiting) the consumption of fruit, nuts, seeds, and dairy.

The DIRTY, LAZY, KETO Food Pyramid is not a defined, step-by-step prescription; instead, it's a reference tool. Looking at a "day in the life" of DIRTY, LAZY, KETO, you will hopefully be inspired about how to distribute your carbs across the food groups. By no means do you have to eat these exact foods. This is just a *sample* recommendation of how your net carbs might be enjoyed on a given day, given a range of 20–50 grams of net carbs, to maximize your ability to lose weight.

Go with the Flow

I remember asking my family doctor to give me tips for maintaining my 140-pound weight loss. (I was nervous about what to do in "maintenance," as I had never been to this mysterious land before.) I expected him to spout out important biological facts and cite "scientifical" references, but he did none of the above. In fact, his answer stunned me with its simplicity.

"Keep doin' what you're doin' and you'll keep getting what you're getting." (*And this guy went to med school? Okay!*)

Really, his advice was golden. Keep on keeping on when you find what works, and don't look back. Easy-peasy!

The key to making weight loss easy is to repeat good decisions. If you find *eating this or that* helps you lose weight, then stick with it. *Don't poke at it!* If I had a penny for every time someone has asked me "Is this keto?" I'd be a rich lady. How foods affect you is trial and error. Every *body* reacts differently. Drink your Diet Coke, eat a low-carb protein bar, have a sugar-free cocktail (or two!), and see what happens. If these foods cause your weight loss to stall, then cut back or eliminate the offending foods...*at least for a while*. All is not lost; you can try again later.

THE NITTY GRITTY—FINDING THE NET CARBS

Forgive me if you already know how to read nutrition information, but in my experience, a lot of folks can benefit from a quick refresher on how to read it. There's a lot of information packed in a

AVOID

| Bread | Pasta | Sugar | Milk | Corn | Beans | Rice |

TIER 1 **FRUITS, NUTS, AND SEEDS**   EAT JUST A HANDFUL

TIER 2 **FULL-FAT DAIRY**   LIMIT—USE COMMON SENSE

TIER 3 **NIGHTSHADE VEGETABLES**   EAT WITH CAUTION

TIER 4 **NONSTARCHY VEGETABLES, HEALTHY FATS, LEAN PROTEINS**   WILL HELP KEEP YOU FULL

TIPS
Eat lots of nonstarchy vegetables!
Eat fats with your vegetables to make them more enjoyable.
Use fat only for satiety and satisfaction, not as a goal or as a food group.

DRINKS

| Water | Diet Soda | Tea | Coffee | Dry Wine | Spirits |

food label, and most of the details are quite confusing! Let's ignore the percentages (too much math) and zero in on what's most important for our purposes—finding the amount of net carbs.

MEET MR. NET CARBOHYDRATE

1 First, notice the serving size.
2 Find the Total Carbohydrate number.
3 Subtract the amount of Dietary Fiber.
4 Subtract the amount of Sugar Alcohols (if applicable).
5 The result is the NET CARBS per serving.

Here's an example:

Nutrition Facts

Serving Size 1/2 Cup (64g)
Servings Per Container 4

Amount Per Serving

Calories 80	Calories from Fat 25
	% Daily Value*
Total Fat 2.5g	**4%**
Saturated Fat 1.5g	**8%**
Trans Fat 0g	
Cholesterol 45mg	**15%**
Sodium 110mg	**5%**
Total Carbohydrate 13g	**4%**
Dietary Fiber 2g	**8%**
Sugars 6g	
Sugar Alcohol 5g	
Protein 5g	**10%**
Vitamin A 2%	Vitamin C 0%
Calcium 10%	Iron 2%

*Percent Daily Values are based on a 2,000 calorie diet.

13
−2
−5
(6)

Paying attention to serving size is key. As you can see in the previous example, the amount 6g net carbs is based on a ½-cup serving. If you were to eat two servings, or 1 cup, of this mysterious food, your net carb intake would double to 12 grams. *That's a big difference!*

End Runs and Magical Math

You might be wondering, "Why are grams of **fiber** and **sugar alcohols** *subtracted?*"

There is nothing sneaky going on here, I assure you. Sugar alcohols (notice I didn't say *sugar*) and fiber are subtracted because these ingredients are not digested by the body. They quickly move through the digestive system as waste. Examples of **soluble** and **insoluble** high-fiber foods include fruits, vegetables, nuts, and seeds. Sugar alcohols are often found in sugar substitutes (erythritol, maltitol, sorbitol) and are used to make sugar-free candies or other low-carb desserts taste sweet.

Now, before you get any crazy ideas with this information, let me stop you in your tracks. I already know what you're thinking, folks—I'm two steps ahead of you here. You won't be the first person to come up with the notion to add sugar alcohols or fiber to all of your meals in order to subtract your way to weight loss. *That's not how this works!* Sprinkling Metamucil on your meals is not an end run to achieving your goal (not to mention it would taste yucky). Furthermore, eating excessive amounts of foods rich in sugar alcohols (think low-carb ice cream) will eventually lead to weight gain, not loss, and cause a seriously upset stomach. Sugar-free desserts, though technically low in net carbs, are usually overloaded in calories. Again, there are no shortcuts, people. *Not a one.*

There is a better way. You don't need to try and cheat the system. I'm going to teach you a healthier method to lose weight and keep it off for the rest of your life. Join me by getting off the emotional weight loss roller coaster. I'll help you learn how to eat "normally" *for good.* Don't worry—I'm going to hold your hand and carefully walk you through every step. That's an easy-peasy promise. Let's do this together.

CHAPTER 2

KITCHEN INSPECTION

DOES YOUR KITCHEN HAVE WHAT IT TAKES?

Let's get started with touring the most important room in your house—*the kitchen*. I promise not to judge any outdated appliances or scoff at chipped dishes (that's how they look at my house!). As I've said many times before, with DIRTY, LAZY, KETO, you don't need anything fancy to be successful. Beyond a positive attitude, all you really need are the basics. By the end of this chapter, you'll have two specific lists for how to get started: a wish list for any missing kitchen utensils and a short food list to take to the grocery store.

KITCHEN TOOLS AND GADGETS

Before you get started cooking, take time to clear out the clutter from your kitchen drawers. Remove duplicates and broken utensils taking up valuable space. Make notes about items that are screaming to be upgraded. Carefully organize what's left.

> Set the stage for easy-peasy cooking and let the culinary magic begin!

Making a List and Checking It Twice

Do you have to have everything on this list? Probably not. I'm sure a towel can fill in for a set of hot pads in a pinch. For my overachievers, though, I wanted to provide a complete list of the kitchen utensils and products frequently called for throughout this cookbook. If you're looking to upgrade or purchase some of these items, be sure to choose the silicone versions, which make cleanup a snap! I've also placed an asterisk (*) next to optional items, which I understand you may or may not have. You don't have to worry (or max out your credit card trying to buy them all). Your trusty oven or old-fashioned knife and cutting board still do the trick!

- Air fryer*
- Aluminum foil
- Baking dish (9" × 13")
- Baking dish (9" × 9")
- Baking sheet
- Blender
- Can opener
- Cast iron skillet
- Cheese grater
- Cutting board or nonstick cutting mat
- Food processor*
- Grill, outdoor*
- Hot pads (set)
- Ice cream scoop
- Immersion blender*
- Julienne peeler
- Kitchen timer
- Knife set (sharpened)
- Loaf pan (9" × 5")
- Measuring cups (set)
- Measuring spoons (set)
- Measuring tape
- Meat thermometer
- Mixer (or strong arms)
- Mixing bowls (set)
- Muffin pan
- Parchment paper
- Pitcher
- Pizza cutter
- Pizza pan (14")
- Plastic wrap
- Pressure cooker*
- Rolling pin
- Saucepan with lid
- Soup pot with lid
- Scraper
- Skewers
- Skillet, nonstick (large)
- Skillet, nonstick (small)
- Slow cooker*
- Spatula
- Spoon (large, slotted)
- Spoon (large, wooden)
- Tongs, metal
- Toothpicks
- Vegetable peeler
- Waffle maker
- Whisk
- Wine opener
- Wire baking rack

THE BARE MINIMUM

To be a successful DLK home cook, you'll need to stock your kitchen with a few keto necessities. No, you won't need to buy anything unusual or expensive. That's not my style! In fact, I've pared down my recommendations to include only the absolute essentials needed to make the recipes in this book. First, we'll cover pantry staples and then commonly used cooking ingredients.

> Home cooking doesn't have to be complicated or take all day—that's an easy-peasy promise!

Using five main ingredients (or less), I'll teach you how to quickly put together healthy meals and snacks. Why did I choose five, you might ask? My answer might prove to be somewhat embarrassing. Without a written grocery list in hand, my old-lady brain can only be depended upon to remember about five ingredients to buy at the store (any more than five and I'm likely to forget something). *There you go!*

I'm going to assume you keep some standard ingredients on hand (like salt and pepper). I won't be counting pantry staples like this in the five main ingredients used to build each recipe. Following, you'll find a short list of other assumed "freebies" (ingredients you most likely keep stocked in your cupboard). If any of these items are missing from your pantry, now's the time to start a list. You'll want to keep a permanent supply on hand of the following ten ingredients. In the recipes, you'll see these pantry staples called out with a yellow star.

ASSUMED PANTRY STAPLES

- **Salt**—Buy whatever salt you prefer. In keto land, there's a lot of debate about what the best salt is (Himalayan, sea salt, and so on), which I find humorous. Personally, I don't see a difference (unless you're talking about margaritas). In my book, salt is salt is salt.
- **Ground black pepper**—Some die-hard keto folks avoid spices like pepper because of the empty carbs. You might be surprised to learn that black pepper has 1g net carbs per 1-teaspoon serving. Come on, people. What will we worry about next? First

black pepper, then toothpaste. Let it go already. Who puts an entire teaspoon of black pepper on their one serving anyway?

- **Superfine blanched almond flour**—When it comes to shopping for almond flour, look carefully at the nutrition label. There is a wide variety of net carb counts among the different brands. I prefer superfine blanched almond flour with 3g net carbs per ¼-cup serving. I buy this in bulk at Costco.

- **Baking powder**—Check the expiration date of your baking powder often, as this can affect its potency. No one wants deflated bread. *That would be sad.*

- **Garlic powder**—Cooking with garlic powder (versus fresh garlic) is a point of contention made by the keto police, as fresh garlic has fewer grams of net carbs per serving. I'm not going to argue with the food police about garlic. This here is lazy keto, folks. I like to cut corners sometimes! All that peeling and chopping of garlic is exhausting and makes my fingers smell (the struggle is real). I want to make keto cooking easier (and less stinky) for you—this is an easy-peasy cookbook after all—so we're going to make do with garlic powder.

- **Olive oil**—Use whichever oil you are most comfortable with. I mostly frequently use olive oil in my cooking because of its bland, almost universal application. Plus, it always seems to be on sale.

- **Pure vanilla extract**—The pure stuff too pricey for you? I often substitute the cheapie stuff from the dollar store. *Don't judge.*

- **0g net carbs sweetener**—Use the type of sugar-free substitute that you can tolerate and is in line with your personal values. You won't find any criticism here, my friends. But just in case you're curious, for the purposes of calculating macronutrient information here in this cookbook, the nutritionist used Lakanto brand 0g net carbs sweetener (erythritol/monk fruit) in the recipe macronutrient calculations.

- **Vegetable broth**—In lieu of vegetable broth, you may substitute homemade or commercially prepared beef or chicken stock (sold in cans or cartons or made with bouillon cubes). I encourage you to customize recipes in line with your tastes. In this cookbook, the nutritional information for recipes using broth is calculated based on 1g net carbs per 1-cup serving of vegetarian-style broth.

- **Sugar-free chocolate chips**—Don't laugh, but I think chocolate chips are a pantry staple! At least in my house, I take chocolate cravings seriously—*I don't want to be caught slippin'*. No matter what the recipe is, I'm prepared to sprinkle sugar-free chocolate chips on top. ChocZero, Lily's, and Hershey's all make different types of suitable sugar-free chocolate chips. The nutritionist here used Lily's brand chocolate chips when calculating macronutrients in applicable recipes.

GROCERY SHOPPING LIST

Now that your kitchen is set up for easy-peasy cooking, it's time for a quick trip to the supermarket.

> Included here you'll find a quick, beginner DIRTY, LAZY, KETO grocery list to help get you started.

You don't need to buy everything on this list—these are just recommendations. The **pantry staples** discussed earlier are designated with **bold font**. You don't ever want to get low on these frequently used DLK ingredients. Lastly, before heading out to the grocery store, don't forget to jot down additional ingredients needed for upcoming meals. Add those items to the bottom of your list.

DRINKS (ALL SUGAR-FREE)
- ❏ Coffee (unsweetened)
- ❏ Diet soda
- ❏ Energy drinks
- ❏ Flavor packets (or squirts) to add to water
- ❏ Sports drinks with electrolytes
- ❏ Tea, unsweetened (herbal and black)
- ❏ Water (plain, sparkling, and flavored)

MEATS (WITHOUT SUGAR ADDITIVES)
- ❏ Alternative Protein: soy foods (tofu, black soy beans)
- ❏ Bacon
- ❏ Deli meat
- ❏ Sausage
- ❏ Seafood

DAIRY

❏ Butter
❏ Canned dairy whipped topping (unsweetened)
❏ Cheese (all kinds, full-fat)
❏ Cream cheese (full-fat)
❏ Dairy alternative milk (for example, almond milk, unsweetened)
❏ Eggs
❏ Half and half (full-fat)
❏ Heavy whipping cream
❏ Sour cream (full-fat)
❏ Yogurt (full-fat, plain, Greek-style)

PRODUCE

❏ Avocados
❏ Broccoli
❏ Cabbage
❏ Cauliflower
❏ Celery
❏ Salad mix

MISCELLANEOUS

❏ **0g net carbs sweetener**
❏ **Baking powder**
❏ Baking soda
❏ **Black pepper (ground)**
❏ **Broth (vegetarian)**
❏ Candy (hard, sugar-free)
❏ **Chocolate chips (sugar-free)**
❏ Cinnamon
❏ Cocoa powder (100%)
❏ Coconut (unsweetened, shredded)
❏ Coconut flour
❏ Coconut milk (canned, unsweetened, 12%–14% fat)
❏ Creole seasoning mix
❏ **Superfine blanched almond flour**
❏ **Garlic powder**
❏ Gelatin (sugar-free, flavored and unflavored)
❏ Hot sauce
❏ Italian seasoning
❏ Lemon juice (100%)

- ❏ Lime juice (100%)
- ❏ Marinara sauce (no-sugar-added)
- ❏ Mayonnaise (full-fat)
- ❏ Nut butter (no-sugar-added)
- ❏ **Olive oil**
- ❏ Olives
- ❏ Pancake syrup (sugar-free)
- ❏ Parmesan cheese (grated)
- ❏ Pork rinds
- ❏ Protein powder (low-carb)
- ❏ Pickles
- ❏ Ranch seasoning mix
- ❏ Salad dressing (suggestion: ranch or blue cheese)
- ❏ **Salt**
- ❏ Soy sauce
- ❏ Taco powder seasoning mix
- ❏ Tortillas (low-carb)
- ❏ Vinegar (white and apple cider)
- ❏ **Vanilla extract, pure**

> Need tips on picking the perfect DLK yogurt?
> Watch helpful videos about this and more at:
> www.youtube.com/c/DIRTYLAZYKETOStephanieLaska.

CHAPTER 3

CAREFREE COOKIN'

MAKE DLK GOOF-PROOF

Making mouthwatering meals doesn't have to be complicated. I want to remove any and all barriers stopping you from cooking healthy meals. *The DIRTY, LAZY, KETO® 5-Ingredient Cookbook* is here to simplify your path to weight loss success. That's my easy-peasy promise!

TOP TO BOTTOM

To make sure we're on the same page, let's stop for a moment and talk about the recipes themselves. Prior to writing my first cookbook, I had no idea there was a rhyme or reason to how a recipe was laid out. I would be halfway done trying to make a snack before realizing I lacked a critical ingredient, gadget, or worse, enough time to finish the recipe (marinate overnight? but I'm hungry now!).

Let's prevent these unfortunate scenarios from happening to you. I want to talk about the importance of reviewing the entire recipe *before you start cooking*. To be clear, you'll need to read the whole thing. *Yes, every part!* This isn't pointless homework. Understanding the benefits of each recipe section can be a DLK game changer. Your keto confidence in the kitchen will soar.

START AT THE BEGINNING

If you're like most people, you decide which recipe to make by flipping through the pages, hunting for a yummy picture to catch your eye. Birthday cake for dinner? *Looks good!* I love the pictures too. But there are other methods you might not yet have considered. I'd like to introduce you to two new strategies: matching recipe icons to your immediate needs and selecting a recipe based on its listed net carb count. Take my suggestions with a grain of salt, but I expect they will be useful for staying on track (when compared to drooling over a birthday cake). *Just sayin'.*

DLK IS ICONIC

Below each recipe's title, you'll find an assortment of cute little icons. *No, I wasn't doodling random pictures.* As you recall from reading this cookbook's introduction, these icons provide insight about the recipe—who it's designed for and the circumstances it fits best. For example, you might want a snack that doesn't require much effort. The No Cook icon directs you to a recipe you can quickly mix, fix, and enjoy! (Perfect for when you're feeling ultra lazy.) And what if you're really hungry? There's an icon for that too—appropriately called, I'm Hangry! Whether you're serving picky eaters, guests, or pseudo-vegetarians, the icons will point you in the right direction for what recipe to make. Think of these icons as recommendations from a friend.

"Oh, you're having company over tonight? Try serving this.…"

Helpful, right?

SPEND CARBS WISELY

Another strategy for figuring out what to eat is to look at the net carb count per serving of each recipe. Thankfully, all of the math has been done for you here. The amount of net carbs per serving is clearly written in the top corner of each recipe (along with the complete nutritional breakdown). *You're welcome!* This strategy is extra helpful when it's the end of the day and you're just about out of your daily allotment of carbs to spend. Using the carb count as a guide, you can easily hunt for a recipe with, let's say, only 1 or 2 grams of net carbs per serving.

Despite having the serving size information spelled out for every recipe, some folks still get confused. I can't tell you how many emails I've fielded from readers all asking the same question: "How much of the recipe can I eat for that amount of carbs—the entire recipe?" I'd like to field that question once and for all.

> **The amount of net carbs listed is for *one* serving of the recipe (not the whole thing).**

Just below the net carb count for each recipe is the **yield**, or number of servings that the recipe makes.

> Divide the total recipe quantity by the **yield** to determine the serving size. So, if a lasagna serves eight people and has 9g of net carbs per serving, cut your lasagna into eight even pieces and enjoy your one serving with 9g net carbs. *Easy-peasy!*

I suspect where the confusion lies is the fact that the exact amount of a serving (like 1 cup) is clearly spelled out on nutrition labels but *not* in recipes. *Why is that?* There are too many variables involved with cooking to provide an exact amount. The size of the eggs you use or the weight of your vegetables directly affects how much food is made. But I digress.…Let's not overcomplicate this issue. In the spirit of Lazy Keto, put away your food scales and measuring cups when estimating what portion to serve yourself. If a recipe serves two, eyeball half of what you made, and enjoy!

PREPARE YOURSELF

Every recipe begins with a relevant note about weight loss or keto cooking from yours truly—I want to get you in the mood to cook. I'm here to support you! Once you're feeling properly motivated, move on to review the list of required recipe ingredients. *Notice they are listed in the exact order of when they are used.* I recommend that you read the ingredient list "once, twice, three times a lady" to make sure you have everything you need on hand. Even better, pull the required ingredients out from the cupboards or fridge and place them on the countertop. Now you're ready to go! And because I don't want you to be surprised about how long all of this will take, I've included exactly how many minutes of **prep time** and **cook time** will be required. *No surprises here!*

I encourage you to modify recipes according to your specific tastes. In the **Tips & Options** section located along the side of every recipe page, I make clever suggestions for changing the flavors or making substitutions. Also in this section, if you don't have a recommended cooking gadget (like an air fryer), I offer an alternate cooking method. I hope you're beginning to see how reading through the full recipe will set you up for success! I've got your back, people.

NO MINCED WORDS

My husband and I went to great lengths to make the recipe directions as stress-free as possible. We don't come from a professional culinary background, so forgive us for not using (or knowing!) fancy-pants cooking words. *The DIRTY, LAZY, KETO® 5-Ingredient Cookbook* won't leave you feeling intimidated. We aren't going to be searing, blanching, poaching, or braising here, *no sirree, Bob*. Instead, the plan is to keep directions clear and to the point. Cooking instructions are limited to the basics:

- Bake
- Boil
- Fry
- Grill
- Sauté (Okay, I'll admit that one sounds a little fancy.)
- Simmer
- Steam

SAVE FACE AND EVEN DINNER!

Recipes are a road map to success, but that's only true when they're followed to a T. Even the best of us can become distracted and make a mistake in the kitchen. Mess-ups are a *normal* part of the cooking process. Whether it's a minor skipped step or an overall epic fail, there is always a way to save face (and salvage dinner).

The following are some foolproof tips to help prevent disaster in the first place as well as some easy-peasy cover-up strategies to hide accidental mistakes.

SLOW YOUR ROLL

1 In general, turn the heat down. No one likes burnt food!
2 As a rule, heat the pan first, then add oil. Test to make sure the oil is hot enough before adding ingredients.
3 Measure carefully—*and not* over the mixing bowl (in case an avalanche of spice pours out of the container).

SPREAD IT OUT

1 Food needs room to cook. Don't be stingy with space!
2 Don't crowd your pan, skillet, grill, or baking dish.

TAKE A TASTE TEST

1 When "spicing up" your food, less is more. It's easy to add more heat later but very difficult to tone it down when overdone.
2 Taste your food before serving it to others. This allows you to make a quick adjustment if needed.
3 Take the guesswork out of adding flavors and buy spice blends (Italian, Greek, Mexican, Creole, and so on). The work of balancing each spice is done for you.

LET IT REST

1 Let cooked meat stew in its juices for a few minutes before slicing and serving.
2 When making baked goods, use room temperature eggs and butter.
3 Lasagna will firm up if given a chance. Let a cooked lasagna sit for an hour before cutting and serving. Even better, reheated lasagna (the next day) is at its peak performance.
4 Patiently wait for the oven to preheat. No rushing! Similarly, don't open an oven or slow cooker when it's cooking food. Sneak peaks release a ton of heat (and therefore affect overall cook time).

BETTER SAFE THAN SORRY

1 Kitchen safety should be your first priority. Turn pot handles in, keep cords tucked away, clean up as you go, and toss malfunctioning equipment.

2 Stay put when cooking. Don't leave a fire unattended to check what's on *Netflix*.

3 Stay healthy by cooking and storing food using FDA-recommended guidelines. When in doubt, throw it out.

4 Set backup timers. I can't tell you how many meals I've ruined because of techno glitches.

COVER UP THE EVIDENCE

1 *Too spicy?* Try toning down the heat with dairy (sour cream, heavy whipping cream, or half and half).

2 *Too sweet?* Add a little salt.

3 *Too salty?* Add something sweet.

4 *Not tasting very good?* I recommend adding more fat (butter, cheese, sour cream, bacon). Fat makes everything taste better!

5 When all else fails and disaster strikes…distract your guests from looking at your mistakes with fancy plating, a pretty tablecloth, or my favorite trick: *mood lighting*. They can't judge what they can't see!

THE DIRTY, LAZY, KETO

Recipes

CHAPTER 4

BREAKFAST

I'm going to tell you something a little embarrassing: I sometimes eat the same food for breakfast day after day (week after week!). I repeat the same meal over and over again. The strange part is that this habit doesn't bother me in the slightest.

As a cookbook writer, I should probably be ashamed of myself. With the many low-carb breakfast foods to choose from, why do I keep eating the *same ole, same ole* for multiple meals in a row? It's not that I'm unimaginative; quite the opposite, actually! Sometimes, I feel like having too many choices causes unnecessary anxiety. I can't figure out what I want. I'll spend hours—*hours*—weighing all of my options.

Even when I go out to eat, I'm the last person at the table to place my order. I enjoy hearing what everyone else is having. Apparently, I suffer from breakfast FOMO. (Note: Don't ever take me to one of those chain restaurants with a menu the size of a phone book. We'll be there all day before I make a decision.)

I never get tired of repeating an easy-to-fix breakfast. I'm a busy lady these days, so if I can remove a looming struggle over *what to eat*, I'll gladly oblige, every time. Repetition alleviates my decision fatigue. It also helps me to be better prepared in the kitchen. The ingredients are purchased and waiting for me in the fridge. I can crawl out of bed still half-asleep, because my morning routine is on autopilot.

I'm a no muss, no fuss type of cook when it comes to making breakfast— that's an easy-peasy promise!

NET CARBS

3G

SERVES 12

PER SERVING

CALORIES	176
FAT	14G
PROTEIN	6G
SODIUM	234MG
FIBER	4G
CARBOHYDRATES	11G
NET CARBS	3G
SUGAR	1G
SUGAR ALCOHOL	4G

TIME

PREP TIME:	10 MINUTES
COOK TIME:	20 MINUTES

TIPS & OPTIONS

Chocolate lovers can flex their muscles here. Add 2 tablespoons 100% cocoa powder to the batter for the ultimate double-chocolate muffin.

Not in the mood for chocolate? (I don't know how that's possible, but whatever.) Then gently fold in ½ cup fresh blueberries instead.

CHOCOLATE CHIP MUFFINS IN A JIFFY

Truth be told, I used to regularly buy and make boxed Jiffy muffin and cake mixes from the grocery store. I loved the simplicity of the package directions (and was addicted to the *carboliciousness* of the final product!). Making DLK baked goods from scratch is just as easy. With less than five main ingredients, I'll teach you how to make a lower-carb muffin. These Chocolate Chip Muffins in a Jiffy are just as fast to make and delicious as the boxed mix from the store.

- **2 cups superfine blanched almond flour**
- **¼ cup 0g net carbs sweetener**
- **1 tablespoon baking powder**
- **½ teaspoon salt**
- **½ cup whole milk**
- **2 large eggs, beaten**
- **½ cup sugar-free chocolate chips**

1   Preheat oven to 375°F. Grease two silicone muffin pans.

2   In a large bowl, whisk to combine flour, sweetener, baking powder, and salt.

3   Add milk, eggs, and chocolate chips and stir to thoroughly blend.

4   Evenly add batter to twelve muffin cups and bake 15–20 minutes until a toothpick poked into the center of a muffin comes out dry. Serve warm.

n/a

NET CARBS

1G

SERVES 2

PER SERVING

CALORIES	159
FAT	14G
PROTEIN	4G
SODIUM	89MG
FIBER	4G
CARBOHYDRATES	8G
NET CARBS	1G
SUGAR	0G
SUGAR ALCOHOL	3G

TIME

PREP TIME:	5 MINUTES
COOK TIME:	10 MINUTES

TIPS & OPTIONS

Enjoy with a cup of un-sweetened vanilla almond milk (1g net carbs per 1-cup serving). Silk brand is one of my favorites, but any low-carb dairy alternative milk will do. *Just make sure it's cold!*

JUST A BOWL OF CEREAL

Out of all one hundred recipes I share in *The DIRTY, LAZY, KETO 5-Ingredient Cookbook*, this one gets me the most excited: Just a Bowl of Cereal. That's right, folks. I said CEREAL! Until recently, I hadn't had a real bowl of cereal in almost a decade. On sleepy Sunday mornings, cereal is something I sometimes miss. I refuse to spend an arm and a leg on overpriced "keto" cereal from the Internet (which I've heard is terrible anyway). It may have taken me years to come up with an alternative, but I've finally figured out a scrumptious DLK substitute. *You're welcome, 'Merica!*

1 tablespoon shelled hemp seeds

1 tablespoon shredded unsweetened coconut

2 tablespoons sugar-free maple-flavored syrup

2 tablespoons shelled, roasted, salted sunflower seeds

1 tablespoon coconut oil, melted

1 Preheat oven to 400°F. Line a baking sheet with parchment paper.

2 In a small bowl, whisk all ingredients together.

3 Spread mixture evenly in a very thin layer on the prepared baking sheet, then bake 8–10 minutes until cereal hardens and turns golden brown.

4 Let cool. Crumble and serve immediately in a small bowl topped with an unsweetened dairy alternative milk of your choice.

NO-SKILL SCRAMBLE

Scrambles are one of my DIRTY, LAZY, KETO standbys. They don't require many ingredients to make, and I find creating new combinations really easy to do. Ham and Cheddar, spinach and tomato, or bacon and Swiss? *No problemo.* Changing up the ingredient combinations helps keep eating scrambled eggs interesting. I make it a rule to always keep omelet basics on hand: eggs, bacon, sausage, and an assortment of cheeses. Added vegetables are a bonus! I can throw together a delicious DIRTY, LAZY, KETO breakfast (or any meal, really) without worrying if I have what it takes.

> 1 cup loose lean pork chorizo (not in a casing)
>
> ¼ cup finely chopped red onion
>
> ¾ cup chopped spinach
>
> 4 large eggs, beaten, divided
>
> ½ cup shredded Cheddar cheese, divided
>
> ⅛ teaspoon salt, divided
>
> ⅛ teaspoon ground black pepper, divided

1. In a medium nonstick pan over medium heat, sauté chorizo 10 minutes while stirring regularly until browned completely. Drain any fat.

2. Stir in onion and spinach and cook 7–10 minutes, stirring regularly, until onions are caramelized.

3. Transfer half of the meat-and-vegetable mixture to a medium glass bowl.

4. Stir 2 beaten eggs into pan with meat mixture for 3–5 minutes until eggs are cooked. Remove scrambled mixture to a plate. Evenly top with half of the cheese and half of the salt and pepper.

5. Add remaining meat-and-vegetable mixture and remaining beaten eggs to pan. Stir 3–5 minutes until eggs are cooked. Remove to a plate. Top with remaining cheese, salt, and pepper. Serve warm.

Pantry Staples

salt, ground black pepper

NET CARBS

2G

SERVES 2

PER SERVING	
CALORIES	564
FAT	42G
PROTEIN	36G
SODIUM	1,612MG
FIBER	1G
CARBOHYDRATES	3G
NET CARBS	2G
SUGAR	1G
SUGAR ALCOHOL	0G

TIME

PREP TIME:	5 MINUTES
COOK TIME:	30 MINUTES

TIPS & OPTIONS

What's the difference between a scramble and an omelet, you might ask? In my opinion, it's the pressure to make breakfast look pretty. Do yourself a favor and become a scramble convert. *The messier the presentation, the better!*

PUNK PEANUT BUTTER CHAFFLE

If you want to have a good laugh, watch my popular chaffle-making video on the DIRTY, LAZY, KETO *YouTube* channel. For all the world to see, I taught my podcast cohost, sociology professor Dr. Tamara Sniezek, how to bake her first chaffle. Somehow, we turned making a five-minute recipe into an entertaining viral video. Sure, there was a lot of girlfriend gab going on—we just couldn't help ourselves. I promise making this easy Punk Peanut Butter Chaffle recipe will go a lot faster. *I'll zip my lips.*

> 2 large eggs
>
> ½ cup shredded whole milk mozzarella cheese
>
> ¼ cup no-sugar-added creamy peanut butter
>
> 2 tablespoons 0g net carbs sweetener
>
> ½ teaspoon pure vanilla extract

1 Lightly spray a waffle maker with nonstick cooking spray and preheat.

2 In a medium bowl, stir to combine all ingredients.

3 Distribute batter evenly among four waffle forms and cook 3 minutes. Repeat with remaining batter if necessary. Serve warm.

Pantry Staples

0g net carbs sweetener, pure vanilla extract

NET CARBS

2G

SERVES 4

PER SERVING

CALORIES	172
FAT	13G
PROTEIN	10G
SODIUM	150MG
FIBER	2G
CARBOHYDRATES	7G
NET CARBS	2G
SUGAR	1G
SUGAR ALCOHOL	3G

TIME

PREP TIME:	5 MINUTES
COOK TIME:	3 MINUTES

TIPS & OPTIONS

Recommended toppings are canned dairy whipped topping (unsweetened) and a dusting of 100% cocoa powder. Top with a sprinkle of sugar-free chocolate chips, *if you dare*!

Craving peanut butter and jelly? Serve this topped with a thin spread of Runner-Up Strawberry Syrup (see recipe in this chapter).

This breakfast recipe moonlights as a delicious dessert too, especially when topped with a scoop of Enlightened brand Chocolate Light Ice Cream (4g net carbs per ½-cup serving).

NET CARBS

0G

SERVES 8

PER SERVING

CALORIES	2G
FAT	2G
PROTEIN	0G
SODIUM	0MG
FIBER	0G
CARBOHYDRATES	6G
NET CARBS	0G
SUGAR	0G
SUGAR ALCOHOL	6G

TIME

PREP TIME:	0 MINUTES
COOK TIME:	15 MINUTES

TIPS & OPTIONS ≫

Sugar-free sweeteners tend to crystalize as they cool. Simply reheat syrup (microwaved is fine) to return liquid back to a proper syrupy texture.

If a thin syrup is desired, omit the xanthan gum. On the flip side, if syrup becomes too thick, add drips of water and whisk until desired consistency is achieved.

Serve your syrup on top of Careless Crepes, Monkeyed Around Bread, or Punk Peanut Butter Chaffle (see recipes in this chapter).

GOLDILOCKS'S PANCAKE SYRUP

The quest to find the perfect sugar-free syrup can be a disappointing one. Some are too sweet and others too watery. Others are too expensive or hard to find! I finally got tired of being lost in this Goldilocks's syrup riddle and created my own recipe. To my surprise, I was able to create a syrup "just my size" with just a short list of ingredients.

½ cup water

✦ ½ cup 0g net carbs sweetener

1½ tablespoons unsalted butter

1 teaspoon maple extract

⅛ teaspoon xanthan gum

1   In a small saucepan over medium heat, combine all ingredients. Bring to a boil while whisking.

2   Reduce heat to low and let simmer 7–10 minutes, continuing to whisk often.

3   Serve warm. Syrup will last up to 7 days if properly stored in refrigerator.

HOMEY HONEY-WALNUT CREAM CHEESE

In my previous carboholic life, I was a regular at Panera Bread (so much so that the cashier knew my first name!). Yes, I loved eating fresh bagels, but perhaps even more so, I relished licking their house honey-walnut-flavored cream cheese spread off the knife. As you know, I'm not one to deny a craving. Nowadays, when I desire this sort of *deliciousness*, I whip up a sugar-free version and spread it on just about anything.

1 (8-ounce) package full-fat cream cheese, softened

¼ cup chopped walnuts

3 tablespoons sugar-free maple-flavored syrup

⅛ teaspoon ground cinnamon

1 In a medium bowl, stir to thoroughly combine all ingredients.

2 Cover and refrigerate until ready to serve. Serve chilled.

Pantry Staples

n/a

NET CARBS

2G

SERVES 8

PER SERVING	
CALORIES	124
FAT	11G
PROTEIN	2G
SODIUM	117MG
FIBER	1G
CARBOHYDRATES	4G
NET CARBS	2G
SUGAR	1G
SUGAR ALCOHOL	1G

TIME

PREP TIME:	5 MINUTES
COOK TIME:	0 MINUTES

TIPS & OPTIONS

Enjoy a dollop of this cream cheese inside a Careless Crepe (see recipe in this chapter) or Kinda Cannoli (see Chapter 10).

Not a fan of walnuts? Substitute any low-carb nut. Suggestions include macadamia (2g net carbs per 1-ounce serving), pecan (1g net carbs per 1-ounce serving), or almond (3g net carbs per 1-ounce serving).

superfine blanched
almond flour, 0g net carbs
sweetener

NET CARBS

2G

SERVES 4

PER SERVING

CALORIES	211
FAT	18G
PROTEIN	6G
SODIUM	92MG
FIBER	1G
CARBOHYDRATES	3G
NET CARBS	2G
SUGAR	1G
SUGAR ALCOHOL	0G

TIME

PREP TIME:	10 MINUTES
COOK TIME:	40 MINUTES

TIPS & OPTIONS »

Yummy toppings/fillings
are canned dairy whipped
topping (unsweetened),
sugar-free chocolate chips,
Runner-Up Strawberry
Syrup (see recipe in this
chapter), or berries.

Fill your crepe with a dollop
of folksy Homey Honey-
Walnut Cream Cheese (see
recipe in this chapter).

Prefer a savory crepe? It
might sound weird at first
to stuff a crepe with a savory filling, but trust me on
this one. Gently stuff your
crepe with warmed leftover
turkey meat and a spoonful
of homemade Pesto from
Cool As a Cucumber Pesto
Salad (see Chapter 5).

CARELESS CREPES

When I have more time on my hands, like on the weekends, I enjoy whipping up breakfasts that I consider to be special. Nothing too fancy or elaborate, though. I don't want to shop for a long list of expensive ingredients or spend too much time in the kitchen. I want to roll out of bed and have *instant happiness* for breakfast. This uncomplicated crepe recipe keeps my morning agenda stress-free.

- ¼ cup superfine blanched almond flour
- 2 teaspoons coconut flour
- 2 large eggs
- 4 tablespoons full-fat cream cheese, softened
- 2 tablespoons heavy whipping cream
- 2 (1-gram) packets 0g net carbs sweetener
- 2 tablespoons unsalted butter, divided

1 In a large mixing bowl, combine all ingredients except butter. Using a mixer, mix until well blended.

2 In a medium nonstick skillet over medium heat, melt ½ tablespoon butter. Pour ¼ of the batter into the skillet and cook 3–5 minutes until firm. Flip and cook another 3–5 minutes. Fold in half or quarters depending on size and remove to a plate.

3 Repeat the process until all the batter is used. Serve warm.

RUNNER-UP STRAWBERRY SYRUP

NET CARBS

0G

SERVES 12

PER SERVING	
CALORIES	3
FAT	0G
PROTEIN	0G
SODIUM	0MG
FIBER	1G
CARBOHYDRATES	1G
NET CARBS	0G
SUGAR	0G
SUGAR ALCOHOL	0G

TIME

PREP TIME:	5 MINUTES
COOK TIME:	10 MINUTES

TIPS & OPTIONS »

For a thinner syrup, slowly add drops of water to the pan until desired consistency is achieved.

If you don't have liquid sweetener on hand, you may substitute ¼ cup granular 0g net carbs sweetener instead (but note the texture of the syrup might crystalize somewhat as it cools).

For recipes like this, where I only use a small portion at any given time, I freeze leftovers in an ice cube tray (1 tablespoon per section). I then store the loose cubes in a freezer-grade Ziploc bag, reheating one cube at a time (as needed).

If you've dined at IHOP before, you're familiar with the assorted pancake syrups set on every table. Before I lost 140 pounds, I was an expert in sampling the different flavors. Butterscotch tasted one notch below blueberry, I thought, but strawberry? Strawberry pancake syrup was a close runner-up to traditional maple. Now when I visit IHOP, I ask the waitstaff to bring me the sugar-free pancake syrup (this is really available!). It's common for restaurants to stock sugar-free maple syrup, but they almost never carry sugar-free strawberry syrup. To enjoy a sugar-free fruity syrup, you'll have to make a quick batch of this classic recipe at home.

½ cup water

1 teaspoon 0g net carbs liquid sweetener

¼ teaspoon xanthan gum

½ cup sliced frozen strawberries

1 In a small saucepan over medium heat, combine water, sweetener, and xanthan gum and whisk continually for 5 minutes. Bring almost to a boil and then reduce heat to simmer.

2 Add strawberries and continue whisking another 5 minutes until fruit boils down and syrup thickens.

3 Remove from heat and let cool enough to handle. Serve warm.

LICKETY-SPLIT ACAI BOWL

I'm never going to become one of those perky modern health-nuts (who we all secretly hate). No matter what the purported benefits are, I'm extremely unlikely to down a shot of homegrown wheat grass for breakfast. *Grass is for cows!* Plus, I prefer to eat something sweet when I wake up. Putting together an acai bowl is about as hip as I can get at my age. My recipe only takes a few minutes, uses a handful of everyday ingredients, and leaves me with pep in my step (and no grass between my teeth).

- ¾ cup full-fat, plain, Greek-style yogurt
- ¼ teaspoon acai powder
- ✦ 3 (1-gram) packets 0g net carbs sweetener
- ½ teaspoon chia seeds
- ¼ cup semi-frozen blueberries
- ¼ cup sliced semi-frozen strawberries
- ✦ 1 teaspoon sugar-free chocolate chips

1 In a small bowl, combine all ingredients except chocolate chips and use a fork to mash them together.

2 Sprinkle with chocolate chips and serve immediately.

Pantry Staples

0g net carbs sweetener, sugar-free chocolate chips

NET CARBS

5G

SERVES 2

PER SERVING	
CALORIES	110
FAT	6G
PROTEIN	8G
SODIUM	30MG
FIBER	2G
CARBOHYDRATES	8G
NET CARBS	5G
SUGAR	5G
SUGAR ALCOHOL	1G

TIME

PREP TIME:	3 MINUTES
COOK TIME:	0 MINUTES

« TIPS & OPTIONS

When shopping for yogurt on DIRTY, LAZY, KETO, check the nutrition label carefully. The amount of net carbs and serving size vary widely among the different brands. One of my preferred yogurts is Fage Total All Natural Whole Milk (5% Milkfat) Plain Greek Strained Yogurt. It has 5g net carbs per ¾-cup serving (which happens to be a pretty generous serving size when compared to the competition). No one is going to cheat me!

MONKEYED AROUND BREAD

Every morning, I add two ice cubes to my jumbo cup of coffee so I can slurp it down as fast as possible without burning my tongue. I want my breakfast meal to be just as uncomplicated. Don't let the name of this recipe fool you. I don't monkey around in the morning; this recipe is about as fancy as I get!

- 1½ cups shredded whole milk mozzarella cheese
- 1 cup superfine blanched almond flour
- 1 ounce full-fat cream cheese, softened
- 1 large egg, beaten
- ¼ cup plus 2 tablespoons 0g net carbs sweetener, divided
- ½ tablespoon pure vanilla extract
- 1½ teaspoons ground cinnamon
- Pink Frosting from Stuffed Birthday Cake Surprise (see Chapter 10), without the Runner-Up Strawberry Syrup

1 Preheat oven to 425°F. Grease a 9" Bundt pan.

2 In a large microwave-safe bowl, combine mozzarella, flour, and cream cheese. Microwave 30 seconds and stir until blended. Microwave again 30 seconds and stir. Add egg, 2 tablespoons sweetener, and vanilla. Stir until dough forms.

3 In a small bowl, combine ¼ cup sweetener and cinnamon and stir. Sprinkle 1 teaspoon into the bottom of the Bundt pan.

4 Form the dough into small balls, approximately ¾" in diameter. Roll each ball in sweetener mixture in the bowl, then transfer to the Bundt pan. Press down on the balls to create a compact loaf.

5 Sprinkle remaining sweetener mixture over the dough and briefly spray the top of the dough with nonstick cooking spray (this helps brown the bread).

6 Bake 17–20 minutes until the bread starts to brown. Check doneness by pushing a toothpick into the center of the pan. It's done if the toothpick comes out dry.

7 Remove from the oven. When cool enough to handle, place a dinner plate over the Bundt pan and flip it upside down to remove the loaf from the pan. If the bread breaks apart when being removed from the Bundt pan, form it back into a wreath shape.

8 Frost with Frosting. Serve warm.

Pantry Staples

superfine blanched almond flour, 0g net carbs sweetener, pure vanilla extract

NET CARBS

2G

SERVES 8

PER SERVING	
CALORIES	234
FAT	17G
PROTEIN	9G
SODIUM	181MG
FIBER	2G
CARBOHYDRATES	16G
NET CARBS	2G
SUGAR	1G
SUGAR ALCOHOL	12G

TIME

PREP TIME:	10 MINUTES
COOK TIME:	20 MINUTES

TIPS & OPTIONS

Don't worry if your bread breaks apart when you're removing it from the Bundt pan—that's part of the fun! Omit frosting if not needed or desired.

No Bundt pan? *No worries.* A medium 9" × 9" glass baking dish will do.

Want to take the "wow" factor up to the hilt? Decorate your frosted wreath with fresh raspberries and a couple of mint leaves. *That kind of style earns five stars, baby.*

olive oil, salt, ground black pepper

NET CARBS

3G

SERVES 1

PER SERVING
CALORIES	343
FAT	25G
PROTEIN	16G
SODIUM	626MG
FIBER	7G
CARBOHYDRATES	10G
NET CARBS	3G
SUGAR	0G
SUGAR ALCOHOL	0G

TIME

PREP TIME:	5 MINUTES
COOK TIME:	8 MINUTES

TIPS & OPTIONS »

I use an inexpensive egg slicer from the dollar store to cut my avocado into perfectly shaped moon wedges.

Take a shortcut and microwave a scrambled egg for 45 seconds on high. Be sure to spray the bowl first with nonstick cooking spray. Otherwise, you'll have permanent egg "glue" left on your dish.

Sprinkle this toast with paprika or Everything but the Bagel Seasoning for flair.

In lieu of sliced avocado, jazz up your sandwich with 2 tablespoons of guacamole (store-bought will do) and a few slices of red onion. *Impressive!*

TOWNIE AVOCADO TOAST

I'm not one to eat my words very often, but in this instance, I'm going to admit defeat. In the past, I've cautioned others about relying on low-carb bread substitutes. They are often pricey, hard to find, and don't taste very good! In spite of my warnings, however, I've observed many DLK fans remain committed to buying low-carb bread products. More and more options keep coming to market (many of which taste quite delicious!). For all the die-hard bread fans, this easy-to-make breakfast sandwich is for you.

- ½ tablespoon olive oil
- 1 large egg
- 2 low-carb sandwich thins, a top and bottom
- ½ medium avocado, peeled, pitted, and thinly sliced
- ⅛ teaspoon salt
- ⅛ teaspoon ground black pepper

1   In a small skillet over medium heat, heat oil. Gently crack egg into the pan and cook 3 minutes. Using a spatula, flip egg and cook 2 additional minutes.

2   In a toaster, toast sandwich thins 2–3 minutes until lightly toasted.

3   Place thins on a plate and evenly distribute avocado slices on one half. Top the avocado slices with egg.

4   Season with salt and pepper and carefully put thins together to make a sandwich. Serve warm.

0g net carbs sweetener

NET CARBS

4G

SERVES 1

PER SERVING

CALORIES	153
FAT	7G
PROTEIN	13G
SODIUM	409MG
FIBER	1G
CARBOHYDRATES	5G
NET CARBS	4G
SUGAR	3G
SUGAR ALCOHOL	0G

TIME

PREP TIME: 1 MINUTE
COOK TIME: 30 SECONDS

TIPS & OPTIONS 〉〉

For the lowest-carb style of cottage cheese, select 4% milkfat.

Note that the serving size of cottage cheese is usually ½ cup (which is less than a serving of yogurt).

Small- or large-curd cottage cheese is a matter of preference. Both have the same amount of net carbs per serving. Buy the style you like best.

Avoid cottage cheese that contains fruit mixed in (like pineapple), as this style is high in sugar.

CREATIVE COTTAGE CHEESE

The low-carb community has to be the most creative group of folks I have ever met. When I first heard about folks microwaving cottage cheese, I was appalled (it sounds weird, right?). Then I tried it. *What a surprise!* It's actually delicious. I played around with adding a little of this and a little of that, experimenting with adding savory and sweet flavors. Ultimately, I liked this simple concoction the best. It tastes like warm cinnamon toast on a spoon. *Who knew?*

> ½ cup 4% milkfat cottage cheese
> ¼ teaspoon ground cinnamon
> 3 (1-gram) packets 0g net carbs sweetener
> 1 tablespoon pecan halves

1   In a small microwave-safe glass bowl, mix all ingredients except pecans together. Microwave 30 seconds and stir.

2   Top with pecans and serve warm.

CHAPTER 5

SOUPS AND SALADS

As a child with a hearty appetite, I wanted no part in light fare. A cup of soup or side salad was a small appetizer that would hardly make a dent in my hunger. Where was the main event? *I'll have fish and chips too, thank you very much.*

As an adult, I was encouraged to eat vegetable soup as a "filler" to help me lose weight. It didn't matter what the rationale was; I couldn't tolerate eating it. Despite being decades older and wiser (understanding the value of eating vegetables), I still can't get past the belief that the vegetable soup I was eating tasted like compost. It didn't matter if it was good for me—I just couldn't do it.

> For most of us, figuring out how to make "healthy" food taste better is the million-dollar question. Listen closely, because I've stumbled onto the answer: *Fat is the secret!*

In all its glorious forms—mayonnaise, avocados, oils, or nuts, just to name a few—fat dramatically improves the flavor and taste of food. Suddenly, soups and salads spring to life! Vegetables, and all healthy food for that matter, taste better when fat is added to a recipe.

> Eating more fat is one of the secrets to my weight loss success.

This shouldn't come as a big surprise, but when healthy food tastes better, folks like me are more likely to eat it. With DIRTY, LAZY, KETO, soups and salads are not just tolerable, they taste delicious. My soup recipes are rich, creamy, and mouthwatering. Salads have become crunchy, filling, and surprisingly satisfying—even as a stand-alone entrée. No, it's not DLK magic that I've added to soups and salads…*it's fat*!

The benefits of eating a higher-fat diet are endless. Yes, the food tastes better, but that's just one part. Fat-forward foods are satiating and emotionally gratifying. You don't feel like you're "on a diet" eating a salad served with *extra* portions of creamy dressing. A bowl of creamy soup made with real, full-fat cream cheese? That's decadence, people, *not a diet*.

NAKED TUNA SALAD

Tuna is an often-overlooked protein source. Most of us have a can or two in the cabinet, but when it comes to lunchtime, we forget it's even there. I want you to move those tuna cans front and center, folks. This keto staple is too good to hide! Tuna is portable, affordable, and easy to prepare. Forget about the bread, my friend. You'll soon adapt to prefer tuna salad on top of shredded lettuce or shredded cabbage all by itself. *Lunch is ready!*

1 (5-ounce) can tuna packed in oil, drained

1 medium stalk celery, thinly sliced

½ cup finely chopped red onion

½ medium avocado, peeled, pitted, and thinly sliced

2 tablespoons full-fat mayonnaise

½ teaspoon garlic powder

⅛ teaspoon salt

⅛ teaspoon ground black pepper

1 Add all ingredients to a large salad bowl and toss until combined.

2 Refrigerate until ready to serve. Serve chilled.

Pantry Staples

garlic powder, salt, ground black pepper

NET CARBS

4G

SERVES 2

PER SERVING	
CALORIES	278
FAT	19G
PROTEIN	17G
SODIUM	486MG
FIBER	4G
CARBOHYDRATES	8G
NET CARBS	4G
SUGAR	2G
SUGAR ALCOHOL	0G

TIME

PREP TIME:	10 MINUTES
COOK TIME:	0 MINUTES

TIPS & OPTIONS

For variety, consider adding a chopped hard-boiled egg to the mix. *Really!*

Choose tuna packed in oil (not water). Not only will it taste better, the added fat will help keep you feeling fuller for longer.

TA-DA TOMATO BISQUE

Tomatoes are a "keto-friendly-ish" vegetable to be enjoyed in moderation. *Sad, right?* I, for one, love to eat fresh tomato in and on my DLK meals. I'll gobble down just about anything doused in marina sauce or salsa. But with 4g net carbs per (medium) tomato, I realize tomato carbs add up fast. For me, enjoying a cup of Ta-da Tomato Bisque is such an indulgence. I savor every spoonful!

- 1 tablespoon olive oil
- ½ cup chopped yellow onion
- 1 (28-ounce) can crushed tomatoes, drained
- 3 cups vegetable broth
- 1 tablespoon Italian seasoning
- ½ tablespoon garlic powder
- ¾ teaspoon salt
- ¼ teaspoon ground black pepper
- 1 cup canned unsweetened, 12%–14% fat coconut milk
- ½ teaspoon xanthan gum

1. In a large soup pot over medium heat, heat oil. Add onions and sauté 5 minutes to soften while stirring.

2. Add remaining ingredients except xanthan gum and bring to boil.

3. Using a ladle, remove ¼ cup of the soup mixture and pour it into a small bowl. Add xanthan gum slowly to prevent clumping and whisk until fully dissolved. Pour mixture back into the soup pot and stir.

4. Reduce heat and simmer 30 minutes, stirring regularly.

5. Let cool slightly and blend to your desired consistency using an immersion blender. Serve warm.

NET CARBS

10G

SERVES 6

PER SERVING	
CALORIES	126
FAT	7G
PROTEIN	3G
SODIUM	867MG
FIBER	3G
CARBOHYDRATES	13G
NET CARBS	10G
SUGAR	7G
SUGAR ALCOHOL	0G

TIME

PREP TIME:	10 MINUTES
COOK TIME:	40 MINUTES

TIPS & OPTIONS

Don't overblend with your immersion blender (there is no going back!). A little texture of tomato bits keeps the soup interesting. Gently pulse instead.

If you don't have one of these fancy-pants immersion blender gadgets, carefully transfer hot soup to a blender and mix on low until desired consistency is achieved.

If you're looking to impress the crowd, drizzle each bowl with ½ teaspoon of heavy whipping cream in an artful design. Follow with a sprinkle of freshly chopped parsley.

n/a

NET CARBS

4G

SERVES 4

PER SERVING

CALORIES	160
FAT	8G
PROTEIN	14G
SODIUM	358MG
FIBER	2G
CARBOHYDRATES	6G
NET CARBS	4G
SUGAR	1G
SUGAR ALCOHOL	0G

TIME

PREP TIME:	10 MINUTES
COOK TIME:	0 MINUTES

TIPS & OPTIONS »

If you prefer, in lieu of barbecue sauce, substitute full-fat ranch dressing here.

When I'm out and about, creamy salad dressings like ranch or blue cheese are usually the safest bet to order in restaurants. If the nutrition information is not available for what you order, estimate 2g net carbs per 2-tablespoon serving.

DRIVE-THRU BACON BURGER SALAD

The bunless burger is a keto fast food rite of passage. Throw that bun out the window of your car, and never look back! *That's a figurative suggestion, by the way.* Nowadays, most restaurants will serve you a burger wrapped in lettuce if you ask nicely. I've only had one fast food restaurant turn me down: Burger King! (They serve only shredded lettuce.) This bump in the road didn't stop me from enjoying lunch, though. I used my spork and got creative. Here's what I came up with! Mimic my Drive-Thru Bacon Burger Salad at home...*or on the open road.*

1 (12-ounce) package prewashed salad mix

2 strips no-sugar-added bacon, cooked and crumbled

2 cooked burger patties, chopped

½ cup sugar-free barbecue sauce

2 medium pickles, thinly sliced

1 Add all ingredients to a large salad bowl and toss to mix evenly.

2 Refrigerate until ready to serve. Serve evenly in four bowls.

CHEESY EASY CAULIFLOWER SOUP

I enjoy keto soup recipes like this one year-round to help me maintain my 140-pound weight loss. Tossing a handful of ingredients into a pot takes hardly any effort, making Cheesy Easy Cauliflower Soup ridiculously easy to make. Plus, it tastes *ah-mazing*. With the excuse of not having enough time out of the way, there is no valid reason you can't make dinner tonight. Let's do this!

- 1 tablespoon olive oil
- ¾ cup finely chopped green onion, divided
- 1 (12-ounce) bag cauliflower florets
- 2 teaspoons garlic powder
- 2 cups vegetable broth
- 1 cup heavy whipping cream
- ¼ teaspoon salt
- ¼ teaspoon ground black pepper
- 1½ cups shredded Cheddar cheese, divided

1 Set pressure cooker on Sauté setting, heat oil, then add ½ cup green onion. Sauté 3–4 minutes until soft.

2 Insert trivet and add cauliflower, garlic powder, and broth. Lock lid. Cook on pressure cooker setting at High Pressure 10 minutes. Release pressure and unlock lid.

3 Remove trivet and add cream, salt, pepper, and 1 cup cheese. Stir to combine.

4 Divide into four bowls and top each evenly with remaining cheese and green onion. Serve warm.

Pantry Staples

olive oil, garlic powder, vegetable broth, salt, ground black pepper

NET CARBS

8G

SERVES 4

PER SERVING	
CALORIES	444
FAT	37G
PROTEIN	14G
SODIUM	869MG
FIBER	2G
CARBOHYDRATES	10G
NET CARBS	8G
SUGAR	5G
SUGAR ALCOHOL	0G

TIME

PREP TIME:	10 MINUTES
COOK TIME:	14 MINUTES

TIPS & OPTIONS

Frozen cauliflower florets work perfectly fine here. (It will be pressure cooked anyway.) No one will know if the cauliflower came from the bottom of your freezer.

An alternative method to using a pressure cooker is to cook on the stovetop "old-school-style" using a large stock pot over medium heat.

This recipe just screams to be topped with a pinch of crumbled bacon bits and diced tomato. *Right?*

SOUPER DOUPER CHICKEN SOUP

Pantry Staples

vegetable broth

NET CARBS

6G

SERVES 4

PER SERVING	
CALORIES	388
FAT	28G
PROTEIN	20G
SODIUM	954MG
FIBER	1G
CARBOHYDRATES	7G
NET CARBS	6G
SUGAR	5G
SUGAR ALCOHOL	0G

TIME

PREP TIME:	10 MINUTES
COOK TIME:	35 MINUTES

TIPS & OPTIONS »

I often make this recipe using leftover rotisserie chicken breast. Store-bought "astronaut chickens" really save time! I combine all of the recipe ingredients at the same time and keep the soup warm on the stove. *With that homespun presentation, no one ever suspects my sneaky chicken shortcut.* (P.S.: Be sure to hide the rotisserie chicken package deep in the trash so you don't get caught.)

Sure, warm soup always hits the spot when it's chilly outside, but I've learned to enjoy soup during the summer months too. There might be a heat wave going on outside, but with the AC cranked up, I'm in the mood to cuddle up with a bowl of this easy-to-make Souper Douper Chicken Soup. No matter what the season, DLK soups will become a permanent part of your low-carb meal planning.

1 (10-ounce) can diced tomatoes and green chilies, undrained

2 cups vegetable broth

2 medium (4.2-ounce) boneless, skinless chicken breasts

1 tablespoon taco powder seasoning mix

1 cup heavy whipping cream

¾ cup shredded Cheddar cheese

1 In a medium skillet over medium heat, add diced tomatoes and green chilies, broth, chicken, and taco seasoning. Bring to a boil and then reduce heat to simmer. Cook 20 minutes covered. Stir regularly and flip breasts after 10 minutes.

2 Let cool, then shred chicken using two forks, keeping chicken in the pan. Reheat pan over medium heat. Stir in cream and cheese. Let simmer covered another 10 minutes, stirring regularly.

3 Let cool and then serve warm in four bowls.

CIOPPINO CLOSE ENCOUNTER

One New Year's Eve while I was dating my now-husband, I was invited to a very special meal at his parents' house. They were serving an Italian family favorite, seafood cioppino. When I heard about the menu, I knew I had made the cut. I doubted his mother would invite just anyone over for seafood cioppino! It sounded so fancy to me. I assumed her homemade recipe took hours to concoct, but to my surprise, she put it together in front of me in under 10 minutes. Delectable meals, even those made for special holidays, don't have to take all day. Here's my "close" version of that special meal.

- ¼ cup olive oil
- 1 medium yellow onion, peeled and chopped
- 2 teaspoons garlic powder
- 1 (8-ounce) can no-sugar-added tomato sauce
- 1 tablespoon Italian seasoning
- ½ teaspoon salt
- ¼ teaspoon ground black pepper
- 1½ cups vegetable broth
- 1 cup dry white wine (sauvignon blanc or pinot grigio are lowest in carbs)
- 1 (24-ounce) package frozen cooked seafood mix, thawed and drained

1 Heat oil in a medium soup pot over medium heat. Add onion and sauté 4–5 minutes.

2 Add all remaining ingredients except seafood and stir to combine.

3 Bring to a boil. Reduce heat and let simmer covered 20 minutes. Stir regularly.

4 Add seafood and return to a boil. Reduce heat and let simmer covered 10 minutes. Stir regularly.

5 Remove from heat and let cool. Serve warm.

Pantry Staples

olive oil, garlic powder, salt, ground black pepper, vegetable broth

NET CARBS

4G

SERVES 6

PER SERVING	
CALORIES	238
FAT	11G
PROTEIN	25G
SODIUM	757MG
FIBER	2G
CARBOHYDRATES	6G
NET CARBS	4G
SUGAR	3G
SUGAR ALCOHOL	0G

TIME

PREP TIME:	10 MINUTES
COOK TIME:	40 MINUTES

TIPS & OPTIONS

Traditionally, this Italian dish is served at lunchtime on Christmas Eve. Think of incorporating new low-carb classics like cioppino into your family holiday traditions.

If you are a seafood connoisseur and insist on ONLY quality seafood, here is a tip: Shop for cioppino seafood ingredients about a month prior to making it so you can patiently hunt for sales (and freeze items in anticipation of the big day).

olive oil, garlic powder, 0g net carbs sweetener, vegetable broth, salt, ground black pepper

NET CARBS

9G

SERVES 4

PER SERVING

CALORIES	87
FAT	4G
PROTEIN	1G
SODIUM	1,095MG
FIBER	3G
CARBOHYDRATES	12G
NET CARBS	9G
SUGAR	7G
SUGAR ALCOHOL	0G

TIME

PREP TIME:	10 MINUTES
COOK TIME:	30 MINUTES

TIPS & OPTIONS ≫

Serve pumpkin soup with a sprinkle of fresh parsley (for contrast) and a sprinkle of toasted pepitas (for texture).

If you can't stop yourself from wanting to impress your guests, serve this soup in mini hollowed-out personal pumpkins. *So kitschy!*

UNPRETENTIOUS PUMPKIN SOUP

I recently took a cooking class that benefited a charity. The instructor was a national celebrity, and I have to admit feeling starstruck *and a little nervous.* Those feelings all but disappeared once I received the course shopping list; in fact, I fell off my rocker. The first recipe (for a soup, mind you) required me to purchase a list of (obnoxious) ingredients over two pages long! In my experience, great-tasting recipes don't need to be so complicated. Take my mouthwatering Unpretentious Pumpkin Soup, for example. I've streamlined the flavorful ingredient list to include only the essentials. Stop being pretentious, people.

- 1 tablespoon olive oil
  ½ large yellow onion, peeled and chopped
- ½ teaspoon garlic powder
- 2 (1-gram) packets 0g net carbs sweetener
  1½ cups canned 100% pure pumpkin purée
- 4 cups vegetable broth
  1 tablespoon 100% lemon juice
  ¼ teaspoon grated fresh ginger
- ½ teaspoon salt
- ⅛ teaspoon ground black pepper
  ¼ cup sesame seeds

1 In a large soup pot over medium heat, heat oil. Add onion and sauté 4–5 minutes until soft.

2 Stir in remaining ingredients except sesame seeds and bring to a boil. Reduce heat and simmer while covered for 15 minutes, stirring regularly.

3 In a small skillet over medium heat, toast sesame seeds, stirring regularly until brown, 3–4 minutes.

4 Transfer toasted sesame seeds to pumpkin soup and stir to combine. Divide evenly into bowls and serve warm.

olive oil, vegetable broth, garlic powder, ground black pepper

NET CARBS

5G

SERVES 4

PER SERVING
CALORIES	265
FAT	16G
PROTEIN	23G
SODIUM	788MG
FIBER	1G
CARBOHYDRATES	6G
NET CARBS	5G
SUGAR	4G
SUGAR ALCOHOL	0G

TIME

PREP TIME: 10 MINUTES
COOK TIME: 35 MINUTES

TIPS & OPTIONS ≫

Sprinkle with parsley prior to serving.

If langostino meat or lobster is out of the question, substitute an equal amount of the more commonplace halibut, mahi-mahi, or monkfish. I have to warn you about monkfish, though: *That fish has a face only a mother can love!*

For a thicker soup consistency, whisk ⅛ teaspoon xanthan gum into the broth.

Out of tomato paste? Substitute double the called for amount with no-sugar-added marinara sauce.

LYING LOBSTER CHOWDAH

The price of real lobster varies widely according to where you live. If you are blessed with access to affordable lobster, *lucky you!* (And what time is dinner again? I'll be right over!) If lobster is not in your price range (or it's unavailable in your community), substitute langostino tail meat instead. This low-priced alternative to lobster (from the porcelain crab and hermit crab family) is a fraction of the cost and tastes pretty darn similar.

- **1 tablespoon olive oil**
- **1 cup chopped celery**
- **1 pound frozen langostino tail meat, thawed and drained**
- **2½ cups vegetable broth**
- **½ cup plus 4 teaspoons heavy whipping cream, divided**
- **3 tablespoons tomato paste**
- **1 teaspoon garlic powder**
- **½ tablespoon Italian seasoning**
- **¼ teaspoon ground black pepper**

1 Heat oil in a large soup pot over medium heat. Add celery and sauté 5 minutes while stirring.

2 Add langostino and cover with broth. Boil 10 minutes. Using a slotted spoon, remove langostino from broth and set aside. Keep broth in the pot.

3 To the pot, add ½ cup cream, tomato paste, garlic powder, Italian seasoning, and pepper. Return to a boil, then reduce heat to simmer 15 minutes, stirring often.

4 Return langostino to the soup pot and gently stir, 2–3 minutes.

5 Using a soup ladle, divide the soup into four small bowls. Drizzle with 1 teaspoon cream each. Serve warm.

MISO HUNGRY SOUP

When you're new to DIRTY, LAZY, KETO, the first hurdle to overcome is figuring out what to eat. Dining out complicates decision making even more. What should you order and what restaurants should you go to? After a lot of misguided attempts, I discovered a DIRTY, LAZY, KETO mecca. Apparently, "my people" were sitting around a big table at Benihana! Their hibachi-style grilled chicken and shrimp dinner, served with ginger and wasabi dressing and a cup of miso soup, is simply low-carb menu perfection.

- 1 tablespoon olive oil
- ½ cup chopped mushrooms
- 4 cups vegetable broth
- ¼ cup miso paste
- 6 ounces extra-firm tofu, drained and cut into ¼" cubes
- 1 medium green onion, finely diced

1 In a medium soup pot over medium heat, heat oil. Add mushrooms and sauté 5 minutes.

2 Add broth, miso paste, and tofu to pot. Bring to a boil, then reduce heat to simmer covered for 10 minutes. Stir until miso is dissolved.

3 Using a ladle, evenly transfer soup to six bowls. Top with equal amounts green onion and serve warm.

Pantry Staples

olive oil, vegetable broth

NET CARBS

4G

SERVES 6

PER SERVING	
CALORIES	73
FAT	4G
PROTEIN	4G
SODIUM	1,012MG
FIBER	1G
CARBOHYDRATES	5G
NET CARBS	4G
SUGAR	3G
SUGAR ALCOHOL	0G

TIME

PREP TIME:	5 MINUTES
COOK TIME:	20 MINUTES

TIPS & OPTIONS

I recommend purchasing extra-firm tofu because it keeps its shape better during the cooking process. Be sure to drain your tofu well—let it sit in a colander for at least an hour.

Top with a sprinkle of seaweed flakes or sesame seeds.

Spice up this soup with a smidge of wasabi. Be sure to stir and blend it completely into the soup to prevent an *overwhelmingly pungent* surprise.

ZOOMER'S ZUCCHINI SALAD

Pantry Staples

olive oil, salt, ground black pepper

NET CARBS

3G

SERVES 4

PER SERVING	
CALORIES	106
FAT	8G
PROTEIN	2G
SODIUM	156MG
FIBER	4G
CARBOHYDRATES	7G
NET CARBS	3G
SUGAR	3G
SUGAR ALCOHOL	0G

TIME

PREP TIME:	10 MINUTES
COOK TIME:	0 MINUTES

TIPS & OPTIONS »

Call me strange, but I often sprinkle a packet of 0g net carbs sweetener over my salad. *I know, I know!*

Add a little excitement to your salad. Mix in a cup of those cute mini mozzarella balls you see in the deli section of your supermarket (drain before adding, obviously).

If you're a fresh herb snob (I have to admit I'm starting to fall in love with them), sprinkle a pinch of chopped dill over the bowls before serving.

No lettuce? No problem. Salads mean a lot of things to a lot of people (you'll see what I mean when you check out the Christmas Dessert Salad in Chapter 10). A salad doesn't have to include lettuce! Take this zucchini with avocado recipe, for example. Using a basic vegetable peeler (not a fancy julienne-zoodle gadget), I created this carefree scrumptious starter salad in 10 minutes flat.

2 medium zucchini

1 large avocado, peeled, pitted, and chopped

½ cup halved cherry tomatoes

½ tablespoon white vinegar

½ tablespoon 100% lemon juice

1 tablespoon olive oil

¼ teaspoon salt

⅛ teaspoon ground black pepper

1   Over a large salad bowl, use a vegetable peeler to shave zucchini lengthwise, creating long, thin, curly strips. Add avocado and tomatoes.

2   In a small bowl, whisk together vinegar, lemon juice, oil, salt, and pepper.

3   Pour over salad and gently toss.

4   Refrigerate until ready to serve, then divide evenly into four medium bowls. Serve chilled.

DOWNPOUR PARMESAN DRESSING

I've never been satisfied with the dainty amount of salad dressing served to me in restaurants. It comes in a thimble for cryin' out loud! Please don't recommend I dip my fork in the dressing cup before stabbing the lettuce, as a means to stretch it out. *That's just not going to cut it!* I prefer to flood my entire salad with Downpour Parmesan Dressing, covering every bite. I recognize that's probably overdoing it, but isn't salad dressing the best part?

- ¾ cup full-fat mayonnaise
- ½ cup grated Parmesan cheese
- 3 tablespoons 100% lemon juice
- 1 tablespoon Worcestershire sauce
- 1 tablespoon Dijon mustard
- ⅛ teaspoon salt
- ⅛ teaspoon ground black pepper

Stir to combine all ingredients in a medium bowl. Cover and store in refrigerator until ready to serve over a salad.

Pantry Staples

salt, ground black pepper

NET CARBS

1G

SERVES 12

PER SERVING	
CALORIES	111
FAT	11G
PROTEIN	2G
SODIUM	213MG
FIBER	0G
CARBOHYDRATES	1G
NET CARBS	1G
SUGAR	0G
SUGAR ALCOHOL	0G

TIME

PREP TIME:	5 MINUTES
COOK TIME:	0 MINUTES

TIPS & OPTIONS

Once you see how easy it is to make your own low-carb salad dressing, the store-bought variety (often with corn syrup or added sugar) becomes much less desirable.

For extra kick, add a pinch of wasabi. Not too much, though. Umami is one thing, but burning your tongue off is another!

SCRIMPIN' SHRIMP SALAD

Summertime salads can be as simple or elaborate as you wish. I'm certainly a fan of the "dumpster" method (a bowl of chopped leftover vegetables from the back of my fridge). If I'm looking to make something more elegant (like if I'm serving lunch to a friend), I try to up my game by making this understated Scrimpin' Shrimp Salad. Serving it in avocado boats really increases the wow factor!

Dressing

¼ cup full-fat mayonnaise

1 tablespoon 100% lemon juice

⧫ ⅛ teaspoon salt

⧫ ⅛ teaspoon ground black pepper

Shrimp Salad

2 large avocados, cut in half and pitted (leave skin on)

1 cup extra-small (100–150 count per pound) peeled, deveined, and cooked shrimp

½ cup finely sliced celery

1   In a medium bowl, whisk together all Dressing ingredients.

2   Enlarge the holes left by the pits in the avocados by scooping out some avocado using a spoon. Leave at least a ¼" ring of avocado flesh along the outer edge of the avocados.

3   Combine scooped-out avocado, shrimp, and celery with the Dressing. Stir to mix.

4   Evenly divide shrimp mixture into the holes in each avocado half.

5   Cover with plastic wrap and refrigerate until ready to serve. Serve chilled.

Pantry Staples

salt, ground black pepper

NET CARBS

2G

SERVES 4

PER SERVING

CALORIES	252
FAT	20G
PROTEIN	10G
SODIUM	518MG
FIBER	5G
CARBOHYDRATES	7G
NET CARBS	2G
SUGAR	1G
SUGAR ALCOHOL	0G

TIME

PREP TIME:	5 MINUTES
COOK TIME:	0 MINUTES

TIPS & OPTIONS

Sprinkle the final presentation with tarragon or fresh dill. *Bam!* Now you're a legit chef.

Next time, think about substituting fresh crab meat instead of shrimp. Be sure to buy real crab meat, though, and not imitation (fake crab is full of mystery fillers and added sugar).

Avocado boats can be served with the peel on or off. I, for one, don't have the patience to peel an avocado. I keep the skin on—*deal with it.*

n/a

NET CARBS

4G

SERVES 4

PER SERVING

CALORIES	245
FAT	23G
PROTEIN	5G
SODIUM	784MG
FIBER	1G
CARBOHYDRATES	5G
NET CARBS	4G
SUGAR	2G
SUGAR ALCOHOL	0G

TIME

PREP TIME: 10 MINUTES
COOK TIME: 0 MINUTES

TIPS & OPTIONS ≫

Fun salad toppings include bacon bits or crumbled Catawampus Avocado Chips (see Chapter 6). Either of these make a perfect low-carb substitution for croutons.

Use leftovers of this salad to make Yippee Chicken Gyros (see Chapter 9) for dinner.

Turning this starter salad into a full-fledged meal is easy. Top with the protein of your choice and enjoy!

Make tonight's meal a Mediterranean surf and turf. Top your salad with a butterflied jumbo shrimp and slivers of steak.

PEDESTRIAN MEDITERRANEAN SALAD

Cheese (and dairy in general) can be easy to overeat. It's low in net carbs but calorie dense, making it a food category to enjoy in moderation. Herein lies the dilemma: Cheese makes vegetables taste better (even lettuce). To help me rein in my cheese consumption, I intentionally top salads with strong-flavored varieties like full-fat feta. A small amount adds just the right Mediterranean flavor— but too much, and suddenly my salad *tastes like feet!*

4 cups chopped romaine lettuce

½ cup sliced red onion

½ cup pitted Kalamata olives

½ cup crumbled feta cheese

½ cup Downpour Parmesan Dressing (see recipe in this chapter)

1 Add all ingredients except dressing to large salad bowl and toss.

2 Evenly divide salad onto four dinner plates and top each with 2 tablespoons chilled Downpour Parmesan Dressing. Serve immediately.

PICKLE-TICKLED RANCH DRESSING

In my experience, being in ketosis (fat-burning mode) makes me crave salty foods. I don't look for chips or pretzels to fill that need. Those are too high in carbs! Instead, I enjoy salty treats like pickles, bacon, or broth. I always keep these ingredients on hand. To make good use of popular DIRTY, LAZY, KETO staples like these, I frequently use them in recipes. I know a pickle-flavored salad dressing must sound surprising at first, but this twist on the traditional ranch flavor packs a powerful punch.

¼ cup full-fat sour cream

2 tablespoons full-fat mayonnaise

2½ tablespoons pickle juice

¼ teaspoon finely chopped fresh dill

¼ teaspoon onion powder

½ teaspoon garlic powder

¼ teaspoon salt

⅛ teaspoon ground black pepper

1 In a medium bowl, whisk to combine all ingredients.

2 Cover and refrigerate. Serve chilled as a dressing or dip.

Pantry Staples

garlic powder, salt, ground black pepper

NET CARBS

2G

SERVES 4

PER SERVING

CALORIES	77
FAT	8G
PROTEIN	0G
SODIUM	327MG
FIBER	0G
CARBOHYDRATES	2G
NET CARBS	2G
SUGAR	0G
SUGAR ALCOHOL	0G

TIME

PREP TIME:	5 MINUTES
COOK TIME:	0 MINUTES

TIPS & OPTIONS

Draw the pickle juice needed for this recipe from the homespun Fickle Pickles (see Chapter 8).

Top the dip or salad dressing with crunchy bacon bits, diced jalapeño, or chopped green onion.

COLD NOODLE-ISH SALAD

Who says you have to cook zoodles? One busy day when I was pressed for time, I delighted myself with this fresh, no-cook discovery. Zoodles, or zucchini noodles, taste great (and look beautiful) in raw spindly form. Just like traditional pasta noodles, zoodles hold their own in a cold salad recipe. Toss with your favorite bottled salad dressing or give my recipe a whirl. This delectable, tangy sauce is no trouble at all to make.

Dressing

3 tablespoons full-fat mayonnaise

1 teaspoon 100% lemon juice

3 (1-gram) packets 0g net carbs sweetener

Salad

1 large zucchini, peeled into zoodles with a julienne peeler

2 tablespoons seeded and finely chopped red bell pepper

1 tablespoon crushed dry-roasted, salted peanuts

1   In a medium bowl, whisk together all Dressing ingredients.

2   Add zoodles to Dressing and toss to coat.

3   Split into two serving bowls and top with equal amounts bell pepper and peanuts. Serve cold.

olive oil, garlic powder, salt, ground black pepper

NET CARBS

6G

SERVES 8

PER SERVING

CALORIES	190
FAT	17G
PROTEIN	3G
SODIUM	209MG
FIBER	1G
CARBOHYDRATES	7G
NET CARBS	6G
SUGAR	3G
SUGAR ALCOHOL	0G

TIME

PREP TIME:	15 MINUTES
COOK TIME:	0 MINUTES

TIPS & OPTIONS »

Instead of getting a separate bowl dirty, if you're serving right away, add the sliced cucumber to the blender and coat it with Pesto. Serve the salad right from the blender. Just be sure NOT to turn the blender on!

Jazz up this salad by adding fresh tomato, feta cheese, black olives, and/or salami slices.

Make extra Pesto for Skedaddlin' Shrimp Scampi (see Chapter 9), to top Tree Hugger Pizza Crust (see Chapter 7), or to stuff a Careless Crepe (see Chapter 4).

COOL AS A CUCUMBER PESTO SALAD

Fans of DIRTY, LAZY, KETO often hear me recommend using fat to make healthy food taste better. *But what does that mean, exactly?* Vegetables taste a heck of a lot better when prepared using butter, nuts, or oil. That's not surprising, right? Fat tastes good! Cool As a Cucumber Pesto Salad is a perfect example. In my experience, I'm more likely to consume a bounty of vegetables throughout the day when eating them doesn't feel like punishment.

Pesto

- ½ cup olive oil
- ¼ cup pine nuts
- ¼ cup grated Parmesan cheese
- 2 cups packed fresh basil leaves
- ½ tablespoon garlic powder
- ½ teaspoon salt
- ⅛ teaspoon ground black pepper

Salad

- 4 large cucumbers, quartered lengthwise and sliced
- 2 tablespoons drained and diced sun-dried tomatoes packed in oil

1 Add all Pesto ingredients to a blender and pulse 30–60 seconds. Scrape sides with a spatula and pulse another 30–60 seconds until smooth.

2 Add cucumbers to a large bowl and top with Pesto. Stir until cucumbers are fully coated. Sprinkle with sun-dried tomatoes.

3 Refrigerate until ready to serve. Serve chilled.

CHAPTER 6

SNACKS

At any given time, I keep an embarrassing number of snacks on hand. You see, I don't want to be caught off guard. A walk to the mailbox? I might get hungry; I better pack a snack. Okay, I might be exaggerating a little there.…*Or am I?*

> You see, one of the secrets to my weight loss success is that I plan ahead. I stock my kitchen (and purse) with the foods I need to stay on track.

All jokes aside, I want to instill in you the value of having quick, healthy DIRTY, LAZY, KETO snacks on hand for your weight loss journey.

> When your fridge or pantry is stocked with the ingredients needed to prepare a satisfying snack, you're a thousand times more likely to be successful in reaching your goals. That's a mathematical fact!

The trick is to figure out *what works for you* and then stick with it. Convenience, cost, and simplicity matter when identifying your go-to snack foods. Availability matters too. Your goal is to make healthy eating accessible and easy. Remove potential barriers blocking your path to success.

Avoid depending on expensive snacks that require a special order or take a lot of effort to make.

Also, snacks shouldn't be complicated. The fewer ingredients, the better! A twelve-layer dip sounds good on paper, but how long will that take you to make? Executing a complex recipe is easier said than done. At my house, just finding a long list of ingredients (or the specialty equipment needed to make said recipe) could take all day. When I'm hungry (*or hangry!*), I need a simple snack fast…*or else.*

The clock is ticking during a "snack attack." There is an urgency to finding a quick DLK solution within a small window of time (or else you risk the hunger beast escaping and going rogue!). The recipes shared in this chapter won't leave you hanging out to dry. They're delicious, are on plan, and can be executed at lightning speed. You'll be in and out of the kitchen in no time; that's an easy-peasy promise.

WING IT! 🥣 ✕ ◎

Did you know that chicken wings were once considered to be useless trash? For centuries, folks called leftover wings *worthless*. That's just mean (and wrong). The formerly bullied past of the chicken wing makes me love it even more. History aside, chicken wings are a popular low-carb snack with DIRTY, LAZY, KETO fans because they are inexpensive, cook rather quickly, and can be prepared in a multitude of ways. Just wing it! There are a million and one ways to flavor and spice up chicken wings—twice dipped is one of my all-time favorites.

> **2 large eggs, beaten**
> **¼ cup heavy whipping cream**
> ✦ **¼ teaspoon salt**
> ✦ **⅛ teaspoon ground black pepper**
> **⅛ teaspoon chili powder**
> **1 pound chicken wing sections**
> **2 ounces ground pork rinds**

1   Preheat oven to 375°F. Line a baking sheet with parchment paper.

2   In a large bowl, stir to combine all ingredients except wings and pork rinds. Stir in wings until coated.

3   Spread pork rinds on a large plate. Shake excess batter off wing sections and dredge both sides in rinds.

4   Evenly space wings on the prepared baking sheet so they are not touching. Bake 60 minutes, gently flipping halfway through. Serve warm.

Pantry Staples

salt, ground black pepper

NET CARBS

0G

SERVES 4

PER SERVING	
CALORIES	328
FAT	22G
PROTEIN	29G
SODIUM	355MG
FIBER	0G
CARBOHYDRATES	0G
NET CARBS	0G
SUGAR	0G
SUGAR ALCOHOL	0G

TIME

PREP TIME:	15 MINUTES
COOK TIME:	60 MINUTES

◀◀ TIPS & OPTIONS

Don disposable plastic gloves during the "breading process" to cut down on the *ick factor*.

Assign one hand to transfer wet wings and the other to press in rinds. Strategic separation of the two helps prevent a gummy buildup.

Pickle-Tickled Ranch Dressing (see Chapter 5) is an excellent dip to cool down these spicy wings.

JALAPEÑO WISPY CHIPS

Pantry Staples

n/a

NET CARBS

2G

SERVES 6

PER SERVING

CALORIES	252
FAT	17G
PROTEIN	18G
SODIUM	714MG
FIBER	0G
CARBOHYDRATES	2G
NET CARBS	2G
SUGAR	0G
SUGAR ALCOHOL	0G

TIME

PREP TIME:	10 MINUTES
COOK TIME:	13 MINUTES

TIPS & OPTIONS »

Are jalapeños too hot to handle? Try substituting snips of green onion or omit this ingredient altogether.

I always feel the need to do a public service announcement about how to safely handle jalapeños. No one wants the dreaded jalapeño fingers (which can burn your eyes or other sensitive areas you might touch after cooking). Be sure to wear food-grade gloves when preparing jalapeños.

Folks new to DLK often worry they don't have access to the "right" foods. They see "everyone" on social media enjoying keto junk food like cheese Whisps and the latest low-carb energy drink and immediately panic. "But my grocery store doesn't sell those!" *Calm down, sir.* Let me remind you that DIRTY, LAZY, KETO does not require you to eat commercially packaged keto junk food. In fact, I discourage it! Real food, from regular grocery stores, is all you need to lose weight. Hold on to your wallet. You can make a delicious batch of salty Jalapeño Wispy Chips at home with ingredients already in your fridge.

1½ cups shredded Parmesan cheese
1½ cups shredded Cheddar cheese
2 medium jalapeños, thinly sliced in rings
6 strips no-sugar-added bacon, cooked and crumbled

1   Preheat oven to 380°F. Line a baking sheet with parchment paper.

2   Put 1-tablespoon-sized mounds of Parmesan on the baking sheet, 1" apart, until all Parmesan is distributed.

3   Top each mound with an equal amount of Cheddar and press down to form compact circles no more than 2" across.

4   Place a jalapeño ring centered on top of each circle. Cover evenly with bacon bits.

5   Bake 10–13 minutes until firm and starting to brown. Serve warm.

Pantry Staples

olive oil, garlic powder, salt, ground black pepper

NET CARBS

3G

SERVES 1

PER SERVING	
CALORIES	145
FAT	13G
PROTEIN	1G
SODIUM	335MG
FIBER	2G
CARBOHYDRATES	5G
NET CARBS	3G
SUGAR	2G
SUGAR ALCOHOL	0G

TIME

PREP TIME:	10 MINUTES
COOK TIME:	13 MINUTES

TIPS & OPTIONS ≫

Radishes are a hearty root vegetable with a long shelf life. Stock up when you catch a good sale. You can toss a bag into your crisper and essentially forget about them until a chip craving hits.

Don't be surprised by the "shrinkage factor." When cooked, radish slices reduce to a fraction of their original size.

Don't have an air fryer? *No problem.* Spread a thin layer of radish chips on a lined baking sheet and bake at 425°F until the desired level of crispiness is reached.

RIDICULOUS RADISH CHIPS

I can't begin to tell you how many heated discussions I've had over the years about radishes. No matter what I say, some folks refuse to believe in their magical power to transform themselves. Since I have the floor, I'll share with you this little secret: If you cook a radish to death (that's a cooking term) and flavor it with plenty of salt and oil, a radish changes into a potato. Still don't believe me? Give Ridiculous Radish Chips a chance. You'll become a radish convert!

> **1 cup thinly sliced (⅛" thick) radishes**
> **1 tablespoon olive oil**
> **1 tablespoon white vinegar**
> **½ teaspoon garlic powder**
> **⅛ teaspoon salt**
> **⅛ teaspoon ground black pepper**
> **1 teaspoon finely chopped fresh parsley**

1 In a medium bowl, add all ingredients except parsley and stir until all radish slices are coated with seasonings.

2 Place in a 380°F air fryer and cook 12–13 minutes. Shake the basket to turn chips halfway through.

3 Let cool slightly, sprinkle with parsley, and serve.

CATAWAMPUS AVOCADO CHIPS

Avocados are the superhero of DIRTY, LAZY, KETO. They're so easy and versatile! I add them to salads, smoothies, and even soups. This fruit (yes, I said fruit!) is packed full of the healthy fat and fiber that help us feel fuller for longer. If you haven't fallen in love with this DLK staple yet (perhaps due to the strange green color or slimy texture?), try eating one in a less familiar form. Enjoy this fun-shaped avocado snack (in disguise)…Catawampus Avocado Chips!

> 2 medium avocados, peeled, pitted, and mashed
>
> 1½ cups shredded Swiss cheese
>
> 2 teaspoons 100% lemon juice
>
> ½ teaspoon garlic powder
>
> ½ teaspoon Italian seasoning
>
> ⅛ teaspoon salt
>
> ⅛ teaspoon ground black pepper
>
> ½ teaspoon paprika

1. Preheat oven to 350°F. Line a baking sheet with parchment paper.

2. In a medium bowl, stir to combine all ingredients except paprika. Scoop teaspoon-sized mounds of the mixture onto the prepared baking sheet, spaced out at least ½" to prevent touching after they are flattened.

3. Spray the back of a serving spoon with nonstick cooking spray and press it into the mounds to flatten each into a catawampus (irregular) shape. Sprinkle "chips" with even amounts of paprika.

4. Bake 21–24 minutes until crispy and starting to brown.

5. Remove from oven, distribute into four small bowls, and serve immediately.

Pantry Staples

garlic powder, salt, ground black pepper

NET CARBS

4G

SERVES 4

PER SERVING

CALORIES	269
FAT	20G
PROTEIN	12G
SODIUM	106MG
FIBER	5G
CARBOHYDRATES	9G
NET CARBS	4G
SUGAR	1G
SUGAR ALCOHOL	0G

TIME

PREP TIME:	10 MINUTES
COOK TIME:	24 MINUTES

TIPS & OPTIONS

Low-carb "chips" like these are easy to overeat—*they're that good*! Portion out personal servings into Ziploc bags as a roadblock to eating the entire batch in one sitting.

Instead of eating these chips as a solo snack, serve them in the place of croutons on top of a fresh green salad.

MOVIE POPPIN' CORN

I went through a lot of ups and downs in my weight loss journey. I'd be lying if I said otherwise! There were two standout moments that almost broke me: the first time I smelled "real" brownies cooking in the oven (oh, the smell of chocolate!) and my first trip to the movie theater without buying popcorn (do they pump the smell of butter into the air vents or what?). Ever since, I've been on a popcorn quest to create a low-carb, effortless alternative. I believe Movie Poppin' Corn is finally it!

1 large head cauliflower, cut into bite-sized florets no bigger than 1"

¼ cup butter-flavored coconut oil, melted

1 tablespoon butter-flavored salt, divided

1 Add cauliflower to a large bowl and top with oil and ½ tablespoon butter-flavored salt. Stir to coat.

2 Add ¼ of the florets to an air fryer crisper tray, spaced out as much as possible. Cook 10 minutes at 400°F, shaking the basket halfway through.

3 Repeat process until all "popcorn" is cooked.

4 Top with remaining butter-flavored salt. Serve warm.

Pantry Staples

n/a

NET CARBS

6G

SERVES 4

PER SERVING

CALORIES	182
FAT	14G
PROTEIN	4G
SODIUM	1,806MG
FIBER	4G
CARBOHYDRATES	10G
NET CARBS	6G
SUGAR	4G
SUGAR ALCOHOL	0G

TIME

PREP TIME:	5 MINUTES
COOK TIME:	40 MINUTES

TIPS & OPTIONS

Products like movie theater salt and butter-flavored oil are sold at everyday grocery stores. Check the area surrounding where popcorn is sold at your grocery store to locate these items.

If your popcorn salt is sold in cumbersome, commercial-sized packaging, decant a small amount into an old salt or pepper shaker.

Remember not to crowd your food when cooking with the air fryer. The space "in between" is where the magic happens!

An alternative to using the air fryer method is to follow the same instructions but bake in the oven at 400°F until crispy.

garlic powder, ground black pepper

PER SERVING
CALORIES	193
FAT	13G
PROTEIN	14G
SODIUM	406MG
FIBER	0G
CARBOHYDRATES	1G
NET CARBS	1G
SUGAR	1G
SUGAR ALCOHOL	0G

TIME

PREP TIME:	15 MINUTES
COOK TIME:	11 MINUTES

TIPS & OPTIONS ⟫

Use whatever type of cheese slice you prefer—pepper jack, for example, will give these taquitos an extra kick!

Dress up your party platter of Teensy-Weensy Taquitos by stabbing each taquito with a toothpick threaded with cherry tomatoes. Sprinkle a teaspoon of chopped parsley over the platter like confetti.

TEENSY-WEENSY TAQUITOS

You might want to make these taquitos when no one else is home. That way, you won't have to share! Good things come in small packages. They look and smell absolutely delicious. Anyone who sees them on your plate will be floored to learn you are losing weight while eating snacks *this good and this pretty*!

4 (1-ounce) deli slices Cheddar cheese

2 ounces full-fat cream cheese, softened

1 (5-ounce) can white meat chicken, drained and shredded

2 tablespoons finely chopped green onion, divided

¼ teaspoon garlic powder

⅛ teaspoon ground black pepper

1 large black olive, sliced

1   Preheat oven to 360°F. Line a baking sheet with parchment paper.

2   Place cheese slices on the prepared baking sheet so none of them are touching.

3   Bake 8–10 minutes until edges start to brown. Remove from heat and set aside until cool enough to handle.

4   In a medium microwave-safe bowl, microwave cream cheese, chicken, 1 tablespoon green onion, garlic powder, and pepper for 1 minute. Stir to blend.

5   Arrange equal amounts of chicken mixture onto each cheese square, making a line from end to end down the center of each slice. Using your fingers, gently pry the edge of one cheese slice off the parchment paper and continue to roll it over the chicken mixture, making a tight tube. Repeat with remaining cheese slices.

6   Press equal amounts of sliced olive on top of each taquito as garnish.

7   Transfer rolls to a serving plate, sprinkle with remaining 1 tablespoon green onion, and serve warm.

FAKE AND BAKE KALE CHIPS

Pantry Staples

olive oil, garlic powder, salt, ground black pepper

NET CARBS

1G

SERVES 8

PER SERVING	
CALORIES	46
FAT	4G
PROTEIN	1G
SODIUM	131MG
FIBER	0G
CARBOHYDRATES	1G
NET CARBS	1G
SUGAR	0G
SUGAR ALCOHOL	0G

TIME

PREP TIME:	10 MINUTES
COOK TIME:	20 MINUTES

TIPS & OPTIONS

If this is your first time prepping kale, take note that the stems and ribs are discarded. Use only the leaves when making these delicate chips.

Add any leftover prepared kale bits to soups, smoothies, or Pesto (see Cool As a Cucumber Pesto Salad in Chapter 5) for a colorful yet *tasteless* nutritional boost.

I'm convinced that with enough salt, fat, or garlic, all healthy food can be made to taste better. Before you get all judgy now, preaching about the benefits of *plain* raw vegetables, let me ask you a question. Have you ever eaten a piece of raw kale? Exactly. Superfoods like kale give healthy eating a bad rap. No one, absolutely NO ONE, likes kale. Chewing on a piece of kale in its raw form is the equivalent of gnawing on rubber bands. Don't suffer like that. Instead, enjoy the health benefits kale can offer you when prepared as yummy chips.

- 2 tablespoons olive oil
- ¼ teaspoon garlic powder
-   ¼ teaspoon Italian seasoning
- ¼ teaspoon salt
- ⅛ teaspoon ground black pepper
-   2 medium bunches kale, remove and dispose of stems and ribs, chop into bite-sized pieces (about 3 cups chopped)
-   ¼ cup grated Parmesan cheese

1 Preheat oven to 300°F. Line a baking sheet with parchment paper.

2 In a medium bowl, whisk together all ingredients except kale and Parmesan.

3 Place kale in a large bowl and top with seasoning mixture. Toss until all leaves are coated.

4 Evenly spread kale on the prepared baking sheet and cook 10 minutes. Turn leaves and bake another 10 minutes until crispy.

5 Let cool slightly, sprinkle evenly with cheese, and serve.

ALWAYS ANTS ON A LOG

Half the battle of losing weight is simply figuring out what to eat. Often, we overthink it! Eating healthy doesn't have to be exotic or elaborate. In fact, sometimes the simplest snacks are the most satisfying. Take Always Ants on a Log, for example. Using everyday ingredients, I typically have on hand, I can always rely on this childhood favorite to fill me up and keep me on track with my weight loss goals.

> **2 (5-ounce) cans tuna packed in oil, drained**
> **¼ cup full-fat mayonnaise**
> **1 tablespoon 100% lemon juice**
> **¼ teaspoon salt**
> **4 medium stalks celery, cut into 3"–4" sections**
> **¼ cup sliced black olives**

1 In a medium bowl, stir to combine all ingredients except celery and olives.

2 Evenly spread tuna mixture on celery, filling the grooves of each stalk.

3 Place several olive slices in a line along the tuna mixture on each stalk. Serve immediately.

NET CARBS

2G

SERVES 4

PER SERVING

CALORIES	222
FAT	16G
PROTEIN	16G
SODIUM	590MG
FIBER	1G
CARBOHYDRATES	3G
NET CARBS	2G
SUGAR	1G
SUGAR ALCOHOL	0G

TIME

PREP TIME:	10 MINUTES
COOK TIME:	0 MINUTES

TIPS & OPTIONS

Swap out the celery for round cucumber slices if you'd like (but you won't be able to call the snack "ants on a log" anymore, and that's half the fun).

Another recipe twist is to substitute no-sugar-added peanut butter dotted with sugar-free chocolate chips to fill your celery boats.

HOKEY HOLIDAY CHEESE BALL

My grandmother habitually served the same foods at family get-togethers. Even if she wasn't in charge of the meal, we could count on her to bring a delicious appetizer. At Christmas, she made the most beautiful holiday cheese ball with green onion, sun-dried tomato, and bacon. She surprised us by shaping it as a Christmas tree, a wreath, or, one year, a snowman! I like to honor her memory by carrying on this holiday tradition, but with a low-carb twist. In addition to the crackers set out for guests, I provide alternatives like celery sticks, cucumber slices, and zucchini spears.

- 8 ounces full-fat cream cheese, softened
- 1 cup shredded Italian cheese blend
- ½ cup finely chopped green onion, divided
- ¼ cup drained and diced sun-dried tomatoes packed in oil
- ½ teaspoon garlic powder
- ½ teaspoon salt
- ⅛ teaspoon ground black pepper
- ½ cup no-sugar-added bacon bits

1. In a large mixing bowl, add cheeses, ¼ cup green onion, tomatoes, garlic powder, salt, and pepper and beat with a mixer until smooth and well combined.

2. Place a large piece of plastic wrap on the counter and scoop out the cheese mixture into a mound on top. Form the plastic wrap around the mixture and shape into a ball. Let cool in refrigerator 1 hour. Set aside remaining ingredients.

3. Prior to serving, spread bacon and remaining green onion on a piece of parchment paper. Roll the unwrapped ball on the mixture until evenly coated. Serve on a fancy holiday plate.

Pantry Staples

garlic powder, salt, ground black pepper

NET CARBS

3G

SERVES 8

PER SERVING	
CALORIES	181
FAT	14G
PROTEIN	9G
SODIUM	513MG
FIBER	0G
CARBOHYDRATES	3G
NET CARBS	3G
SUGAR	1G
SUGAR ALCOHOL	0G

TIME

PREP TIME: 10 MINUTES, PLUS 1 HOUR CHILLING TIME
COOK TIME: 0 MINUTES

TIPS & OPTIONS

Surround this cheese ball with something for everyone to enjoy (carb and low-carb options). Be sure to include a small serving knife. No one likes a double-dipper!

Be creative with your cheese ball shapes and garnishes. A cheese ball snowman comes to life with pretzel stick arms, olive slices for eyes and buttons, and a baby carrot nose.

Reshape leftover portions of the cheese ball and serve it again at the next holiday party. Cover your tracks by "re-rolling" the outside of the cheese ball with bacon bits.

NET CARBS

1G

SERVES 9

PER SERVING

CALORIES	153
FAT	12G
PROTEIN	7G
SODIUM	173MG
FIBER	1G
CARBOHYDRATES	2G
NET CARBS	1G
SUGAR	1G
SUGAR ALCOHOL	0G

TIME

PREP TIME:	10 MINUTES
COOK TIME:	13 MINUTES

TIPS & OPTIONS »

I have found that the finer the grind of the pork rinds, the better they work as a breading. Use a food processor if you have one to get the finest grind.

If pork rinds don't float your boat, try this crunchy alternative. Substitute an equal amount of crunchy textured vegetable protein (TVP). I buy TVP by Bob's Red Mill at 4g net carbs per ¼-cup dry serving.

For this recipe, I recommend buying short, fat peppers. They are easier to seed and stuff.

PRE-PARTY POPPERS

Social events don't have to feel like a keto minefield. As long as you do a little pre-party planning, you'll be A-okay. I always bring a tray of "safe food" to share at gatherings (even when I'm not asked to bring a dish). This strategy helps alleviate the anxiety I sometimes feel when the food being served is out of my control. I feel more confident and relaxed knowing there is a low-carb platter of veggies with dip or a spread of Pre-Party Poppers available to nosh on.

1 cup vegetable oil

18 large jalapeños

6 ounces pepper jack cheese, cut into ¼" slivers

2 large eggs

1 cup ground pork rinds, finely crushed

1 In a medium skillet over medium heat, preheat oil.

2 Cut the tops off each jalapeño. Gently scoop out the seeds and veins using a vegetable peeler blade or other device with a long, thin blade.

3 Fill each jalapeño with cheese and reattach the tops with toothpicks.

4 Crack eggs into a medium shallow bowl and beat. Place pork rinds on a large plate.

5 Roll jalapeños in egg dredge first and then gently press all sides into rinds.

6 Place jalapeños in the skillet and fry 10–13 minutes, flipping halfway through cooking time.

7 Put poppers on a plate lined with paper towels, remove toothpicks, and serve warm.

CHAPTER 7

PIZZA AND BREADS

Pizza and I have had a love-hate relationship that has spanned decades. I could eat slice after slice without hitting a natural stopping point. My bottomless appetite for pizza felt embarrassing.

It's taken me a long time to realize what I really liked about eating pizza. Ironically, it wasn't the melted cheese. I had an aha moment during my weight loss journey that I'd like to share with you.

My family has a tradition of ordering pizza and bread sticks every Friday night. My kids have friends over, neighbors stop by, and the adults enjoy a night off from cooking. I wanted to keep up the tradition, but I didn't want to eat that kind of food anymore. I researched what else I could order (chicken wings and a salad sounded good) and learned how to make lower-carb versions of pizza (*recipes ahead!*). These substitutions worked out and I continued to lose weight without feeling deprived.

One day it occurred to me that it wasn't the pizza or bread sticks that made Friday nights so special at my house. It was the mayhem that I truly enjoyed! Listening to loud music, chatting with neighbors, and watching all of the kids chase each other around with squirt guns was the draw. *Good times.* As a family, we let our hair down on Fridays. We put on swimsuits, wear flip-flops, and use paper plates. Spending time with my family and friends is what I look forward to, NOT the food. *Surprising, right?*

I realized it was the friendships and social situations that surrounded eating the pizza—that was what I truly craved. Better than melted cheese? I think so!

SAY CHEESE CHAFFLE STICKS

Do you pronounce the *a* sound in *chaffle* like *apple*, or the British-sounding way, like in *awful*? (I bet you're talking out loud right now, huh?) My midwestern roots are obvious when I say a word like this. *Potayto, potahto, tomayto, tomahto.* I don't care how you say it; when Say Cheese Chaffle Sticks are being served, I'll be smiling.

¾ cup shredded whole milk mozzarella cheese

¼ cup grated Parmesan cheese

1 large egg, beaten

1 tablespoon superfine blanched almond flour

¼ teaspoon Italian seasoning

⅛ teaspoon garlic powder

⅛ teaspoon salt

¼ cup shredded Cheddar cheese

1   Lightly spray a waffle maker with nonstick cooking spray. Preheat waffle maker.

2   In a medium bowl, mix all ingredients except Cheddar cheese.

3   Fill two waffle molds with batter and cook 3 minutes. Repeat if needed until all the batter is used.

4   Divide the chaffles evenly between two plates and immediately top with equal amounts Cheddar cheese. Tent with aluminum foil and set aside 1–2 minutes until Cheddar has melted.

5   Using a pizza cutter, cut chaffles into ½"–1" strips. Serve warm.

Pantry Staples

superfine blanched almond flour, garlic powder, salt

NET CARBS

4G

SERVES 2

PER SERVING

CALORIES	293
FAT	20G
PROTEIN	20G
SODIUM	759MG
FIBER	0G
CARBOHYDRATES	4G
NET CARBS	4G
SUGAR	1G
SUGAR ALCOHOL	0G

TIME

PREP TIME:	5 MINUTES
COOK TIME:	3 MINUTES

TIPS & OPTIONS

Serve with no-sugar-added pasta sauce for dipping. I buy Hunt's (from the dollar store) or Rao's (from Target or Costco), both 5g net carbs per ½-cup serving.

Never overfill a waffle iron. That's one mistake I've learned (repeatedly) the hard way! Overpouring by even the slightest amount causes the batter to ooze out the sides of the machine. It's a horrific mess to clean up, let me tell you.

garlic powder, salt, ground black pepper

NET CARBS

1G

SERVES 6

PER SERVING

CALORIES	176
FAT	10G
PROTEIN	18G
SODIUM	271MG
FIBER	0G
CARBOHYDRATES	1G
NET CARBS	1G
SUGAR	0G
SUGAR ALCOHOL	0G

TIME

PREP TIME:	10 MINUTES
COOK TIME:	30 MINUTES

TIPS & OPTIONS »

Top your pizza crust with no-sugar-added pasta sauce. Consider Hunt's or Rao's brand pasta sauces, both 5g net carbs per ½-cup serving.

Make tonight's meal a "veggie lovers" pizza. Forgo meaty options (pepperoni, sausage, ham) since the crust is already high in protein.

I keep a package of disposable food-grade gloves in the kitchen for recipes like this. It's much easier to press the chicken into the shape of a pizza crust while wearing proper protective gear.

CLUCK-IT GOOD PIZZA CRUST

You don't have to give up pizza to lose weight. Instead, learn to make it a healthier way. Thankfully, with DIRTY, LAZY, KETO, you've got a ton of appetizing options that are just as satisfying. There are a hundred and one ways you can still get your pizza fix. Cluck-It Good Pizza Crust is just one low-carb idea to get you started.

1 pound (95% lean) ground chicken

1 large egg, beaten

1 cup shredded whole milk mozzarella cheese

½ tablespoon Italian seasoning

¼ teaspoon garlic powder

¼ teaspoon salt

⅛ teaspoon ground black pepper

1   Preheat oven to 400°F. Line a 14" pizza pan with parchment paper.

2   In a large mixing bowl, add all ingredients and stir to combine.

3   Evenly spread "dough" over prepared pan, keeping it no more than ¼" thick.

4   Bake 25–30 minutes until firm and starting to brown.

5   Remove from oven. Crust is now ready for sauce and toppings.

MINUTE BREAD

There comes a point in many a low-carb journey where one MUST have a slice of bread—*or else*! The craving hits and absolutely nothing but a slice of bread will do. The bread craving must be satisfied THIS MINUTE! Are you prepared? Sure, you can keep a loaf of pricey "keto" bread in the freezer for just the occasion; that's certainly an option. I myself don't like to rely on expensive (often hard-to-find) specialty products. Instead, I've learned how to quickly bake a single-serving substitute at home.

- **2½ tablespoons superfine blanched almond flour**
- **1 tablespoon whole flaxseeds**
- **1 large egg, beaten**
- **1½ tablespoons unsalted butter, softened, plus extra for greasing**
- **½ teaspoon baking powder**
- **⅛ teaspoon salt**

1 In a medium greased, microwave-safe bowl, combine all ingredients and mix until well blended.

2 Microwave 1 minute. Gently flip onto a microwave-safe dinner plate (releasing loaf from the bowl) and microwave another 30 seconds. Serve.

Pantry Staples

superfine blanched almond flour, baking powder, salt

NET CARBS

2G

SERVES 1

PER SERVING	
CALORIES	391
FAT	34G
PROTEIN	12G
SODIUM	609MG
FIBER	5G
CARBOHYDRATES	7G
NET CARBS	2G
SUGAR	1G
SUGAR ALCOHOL	0G

TIME

PREP TIME:	5 MINUTES
COOK TIME:	1½ MINUTES

TIPS & OPTIONS

Enjoy your fresh bread, warm from the "oven," with a pat of butter. *Unbelievable, right?*

Drizzle Runner-Up Strawberry Syrup (see Chapter 4) on top and serve at breakfast.

This recipe can also be split to make two mini slices of bread. Just split (wet) dough onto two small greased plates and then microwave separately for 45 seconds first and then 15 seconds after the flip.

NET CARBS
3G

SERVES 2

PER SERVING

CALORIES	312
FAT	26G
PROTEIN	11G
SODIUM	408MG
FIBER	4G
CARBOHYDRATES	7G
NET CARBS	3G
SUGAR	2G
SUGAR ALCOHOL	0G

TIME

PREP TIME:	20 MINUTES
(INCLUDING WAIT TIME)	
COOK TIME:	2 MINUTES

TIPS & OPTIONS

Go ahead, make some extras for later. When a bread craving strikes, you'll be prepared!

Enjoy with a steaming mug of DLK PSL (Pumpkin Spice Latte) (see Chapter 10).

ENGLISH MUFFIN MATES

One of the first things to let go of in a low-carb lifestyle is regular bread. That can be a painful process for some! If you've spent decades of your life enjoying sandwiches for lunch and muffins for breakfast, changing those habits overnight might feel impossible. Be kind to yourself during the transition. Perhaps make substitute breads like these English Muffin Mates for a while. It's okay to ease into your new WOE (way of eating). Think of recipes like this as using training wheels when first learning to ride a bike.

- ⅓ cup superfine blanched almond flour
- 1¼ tablespoons coconut flour
- 1 teaspoon baking powder
- 2 large eggs, beaten
- 2 tablespoons salted butter, melted

1 In a medium bowl, combine all ingredients. Whisk until thoroughly blended.

2 Set batter aside for 10 minutes (which helps it thicken and bake fluffier). *Break time!*

3 Give batter a final stir and pour evenly into two well-greased microwave-safe mugs.

4 Microwave one mug 1 minute and then flip mug onto a plate, releasing the muffin. Cut muffin in half horizontally (when in original orientation as when microwaved) when cool enough to handle.

5 Toast the two halves in a toaster until they start to brown. Serve warm. Repeat process for second mug.

NET CARBS

3G

SERVES 4

PER SERVING	
CALORIES	173
FAT	14G
PROTEIN	7G
SODIUM	534MG
FIBER	16G
CARBOHYDRATES	19G
NET CARBS	3G
SUGAR	1G
SUGAR ALCOHOL	0G

TIME

PREP TIME:	15 MINUTES
COOK TIME:	15 MINUTES

TIPS & OPTIONS »

Serve these with a dip or prepare every cracker as the perfect bite by melting a bit of cheese on top of each one.

Instead of sprinkling table salt on your saltines prior to baking (which arguably disappears), try using a coarse salt for better presentation.

Can you think of a better side to a warm bowl of DIRTY, LAZY, KETO soup (see recipes in Chapter 5)? Aside from eating a low-carb grilled cheese sandwich with a bowl of soup, Sick Day Saltines would be the next best thing.

SICK DAY SALTINES

"What do you eat when you're sick?" is a question I'm frequently asked, which is kind of a strange question, really. I think people are secretly hoping to hear about an "under-the-weather" loophole allowing for ice cream. Sadly, unless you're on your deathbed, a hall pass to overeat carbs (without consequence) doesn't exist. In sickness and in health, I continue to eat the same low-carb foods. If I'm tap-dancing around with an upset tummy, I reach for a couple of these ultra-bland "saltine" crackers instead.

> 1½ cups Carbquik
>
> 2 tablespoons unsalted butter, melted
>
> 4½ tablespoons half and half, divided
>
> ½ teaspoon salt, divided

1 Preheat oven to 420°F. Line a baking sheet with parchment paper and spray with cooking spray.

2 In a large mixing bowl, use a mixer to combine all ingredients except ½ tablespoon half and half and ¼ teaspoon salt. Mix until a dough forms.

3 Place the dough on the prepared baking sheet and add a second piece of parchment paper on top of the dough. Use a rolling pin to roll the dough into a rectangle shape no more than ¼" thick. Remove the top piece of parchment paper.

4 Use a pizza cutter to cut a grid of 2" squares in the dough. Use a fork to create a uniform dotted pattern.

5 Brush the dough with remaining ½ tablespoon half and half and sprinkle with remaining ¼ teaspoon salt. Bake 13–15 minutes until starting to brown.

6 Let cool, remove from parchment paper, and serve warm or cold on a large plate.

PIONEERING PIZZA CRUST

Low-carb pizza dough won't taste the same as crust made with regular flour (wheat). *Know that going in!* I don't want you to be surprised by the change in texture. There might even be an eggy, nutty, or vegetable taste. That's to be expected! Innovative Pioneering Pizza Crust is appetizing in its own (new) way. Give it some time. You might even start to prefer it.

> 3 cups riced cauliflower
>
> 3 cups shredded whole milk mozzarella cheese
>
> 6 tablespoons full-fat cream cheese, softened
>
> 2 large eggs, beaten
>
> 1 cup superfine blanched almond flour
>
> ½ tablespoon Italian seasoning
>
> ½ teaspoon garlic powder
>
> ½ teaspoon salt

1 Preheat oven to 420°F.

2 In a large microwave-safe bowl, microwave cauliflower 4 minutes. When cool enough to handle, transfer to a clean dish towel and squeeze out excess water.

3 Return cauliflower to bowl and add all remaining ingredients. Stir to combine.

4 Evenly press mixture into a *very*-well-greased 12" cast iron skillet. Poke holes in the dough with a fork.

5 Bake 28–30 minutes. Cover with foil when starting to brown.

6 Let cool and remove from the skillet. Transfer to a parchment paper–lined baking sheet and top with desired sauce and toppings.

Pantry Staples

superfine blanched almond flour, garlic powder, salt

NET CARBS

4G

SERVES 6

PER SERVING

CALORIES	372
FAT	27G
PROTEIN	20G
SODIUM	631MG
FIBER	3G
CARBOHYDRATES	7G
NET CARBS	4G
SUGAR	3G
SUGAR ALCOHOL	0G

TIME

PREP TIME:	15 MINUTES
COOK TIME:	34 MINUTES

TIPS & OPTIONS

Instead of wringing out excess moisture with a dish towel (which arguably could be a little gross), pick up an inexpensive package of cheese cloth. I cut off and use only what I need and dispose of the fabric after one use. Follow the same directions using this alternate cloth.

Be sure to generously grease the sides and bottom of the cast iron skillet to make removing the crust easier. Some folks save bacon grease to reuse on occasions such as this.

TREE HUGGER PIZZA CRUST

Call me idealistic, but if a giant, flat, round meal comes out of the oven covered in melted cheese, I'm willing to call it a pizza. Are you willing to take a leap of faith with me? Zucchini deep-dish crust might not have been on your radar until today, but after you take the first bite, I know you'll become a fan. The fact that it's made with so few ingredients will make you love it even more.

3 medium zucchini, shredded

¾ cup shredded whole milk mozzarella cheese

¼ cup grated Parmesan cheese

1 large egg, beaten

1 teaspoon Italian seasoning

 ✦ **¼ teaspoon salt**

 ✦ **⅛ teaspoon ground black pepper**

1 Preheat oven to 400°F. Line a 14" pizza pan with parchment paper.

2 In a large microwave-safe bowl, microwave zucchini 5 minutes. Let cool and place on a clean dish towel. Wrap towel around zucchini and squeeze out excess water.

3 Return zucchini to the bowl and stir in remaining ingredients until well mixed.

4 Transfer the mixture to the prepared pizza pan and cover with a second sheet of parchment paper. Using a rolling pin, roll mixture into a circular shape no more than ¼" thick. Remove the top layer of parchment paper.

5 Bake 20–25 minutes until dry, firm, and starting to brown.

6 Remove from the oven. Crust is now ready for sauce and toppings.

Pantry Staples

salt, ground black pepper

NET CARBS

5G

SERVES 4

PER SERVING

CALORIES	131
FAT	7G
PROTEIN	10G
SODIUM	419MG
FIBER	1G
CARBOHYDRATES	6G
NET CARBS	5G
SUGAR	4G
SUGAR ALCOHOL	0G

TIME

PREP TIME:	30 MINUTES
COOK TIME:	30 MINUTES

TIPS & OPTIONS

A zucchini crust like this is *Instagram* ready. *The color!* Finish it off with no-sugar-added pasta sauce and beautiful bell peppers.

Another surprising option for topping this zucchini crust is Alfredo sauce. Use the provided recipe (see Alfredo Fooled Noodles in Chapter 9) or pick up a premade jar from the store. Purchased Alfredo sauce varies from 1g–3g net carbs per ¼-cup serving depending on the brand.

CHAPTER 8

SIDE DISHES

From a young age, I was taught to take side dishes seriously. I remember driving home from my gram's, listening to my parents talk *on and on* about how Gram cooked the carrots.

"Too much butter," my mom argued. "That's not healthy."

Like many of you who grew up in the eighties, my family climbed aboard the low-fat diet train. Maybe climbed aboard is too gentle a description—I think my family was *run over by the train*. It wasn't long before the contents of our pantry and fridge were replaced by sexier, fat-free substitutes. Chips, cheeses, baked goods, and granola bars *that tasted like cardboard* took the place of their more flavorful, full-fat counterparts. Gram's buttered carrots were permanently removed from our dinner menu—along with all other buttered vegetables. In their place, a menu of fat-free rice, pasta, and baked potatoes (topped with margarine and fat-free sour cream, *aka glue*).

Looking back, I probably spent two decades of my youth feeling hungry. The high-carb side dishes I ate during the fat-free revolution likely contributed to my overeating. I never felt full! Now, with DIRTY, LAZY, KETO, I'm much more in tune with my body's needs.

> I discovered that eating a diet higher in fats is what gives me *more energy*. My stomach doesn't grumble like it used to.

If my gram were alive, I think she'd be proud of me. Like her, I enjoy my vegetables with plenty of butter (or other fat) *when it's needed* to improve their taste. I don't think there's anything wrong with using sensible amounts of butter, oil, cream, or nuts in my cooking. Adding fats to my vegetable side dishes makes them more tolerable, enjoyable even!

> Instead of consuming fat grams to "hit a ratio goal" (like in Strict Keto), I utilize fats to make healthy food like vegetables taste better.

Please don't misunderstand: I don't drown every side dish I make with fat. I know low-carb veggies are good for me and will help me manage my weight, so I'm willing to work hard to make them taste good. For some vegetables, this is a challenge; that's where adding fat comes in! **Consistently eating vegetables (in a variety of ways) is one of the secrets behind my weight loss success.**

FICKLE PICKLES

Combat the mythical keto flu by frequently drinking sips of pickle juice. You heard me right, *pickle juice*! Forget buying commercial sports drinks to restore electrolytes. Ward off leg cramps (an early sign of dehydration) by drinking this flavorful, salty brine. To make sure you always have some on hand, I'll share my lazy pickle-making recipe here. This recipe is a double whammy—you get to eat homemade pickles now and drink the juice later!

5 medium cucumbers, trimmed and quartered lengthwise

¾ cup apple cider vinegar

¾ cup water

1½ tablespoons salt

1 tablespoon minced garlic

1 tablespoon finely chopped fresh dill

1   Place twenty cucumber spears in a large jar.

2   In a medium saucepan over medium heat, combine remaining ingredients except dill. Cook 10 minutes, stirring regularly to dissolve salt. Let cool.

3   Stir in dill. Transfer mixture to the jar, covering the spears until jar is almost full, and tighten the lid.

4   Refrigerate overnight. Serve chilled.

Pantry Staples

salt

NET CARBS

5G

SERVES 10

PER SERVING

CALORIES	22
FAT	0G
PROTEIN	1G
SODIUM	107MG
FIBER	1G
CARBOHYDRATES	6G
NET CARBS	5G
SUGAR	3G
SUGAR ALCOHOL	0G

TIME

PREP TIME:	5 MINUTES, PLUS OVERNIGHT CHILLING TIME
COOK TIME:	10 MINUTES

TIPS & OPTIONS

If you don't plan on giving out kisses tonight, add a teaspoon or two more of garlic to the pickle brine. The added flavor is *incredible*.

Fresh pickles are the crunchiest (over time they become soft and mushy). Get snackin'!

NET CARBS

3G

SERVES 6

PER SERVING

CALORIES	70
FAT	4G
PROTEIN	5G
SODIUM	203MG
FIBER	1G
CARBOHYDRATES	4G
NET CARBS	3G
SUGAR	1G
SUGAR ALCOHOL	0G

TIME

PREP TIME:	5 MINUTES
COOK TIME:	30 MINUTES

TIPS & OPTIONS »

An alternative cooking method is to use the air fryer. Bake 12 minutes at 400°F.

Resist the urge to pour balsamic vinegar over your Brussels sprouts. This sugary condiment weighs in between 2g–5g net carbs per 1-teaspoon serving (depending on brand). Instead, try with a drizzle of Goldilocks's Pancake Syrup (see Chapter 4).

Does your supermarket sell "roided out" Brussels sprouts? Cut those jumbo-sized Brussels sprouts in half to ensure a speedy cook time.

BAMBOOZLING BACON BRUSSELS SPROUTS

One annoying fact about Brussels sprouts is the serving size. Cooked from fresh, ¾ cup Brussels sprouts has 4g net carbs per serving. This amounts to approximately four small balls (which barely whets my appetite). For a green vegetable, this small serving size doesn't seem very fair. I can practically eat a pound of Brussels sprouts in one sitting! There is a lot of debate about whether low-carb vegetables "should count at all" toward one's daily allotment of carbs, to which I respond, "I don't think my weight problems stem from overeating vegetables!"

6 strips no-sugar-added bacon, halved (to make 12 short strips)
12 large Brussels sprouts

1 Preheat oven to 380°F. Line a baking sheet with parchment paper.

2 Spread bacon on the prepared baking sheet and roll up a Brussels sprout in each strip.

3 Bake 25–30 minutes, flipping halfway through cook time, until bacon is crisp and sprouts are softened.

4 Remove from baking sheet and serve warm.

FOMO FRIED GREEN TOMATOES

Making fried food is easy with DIRTY, LAZY, KETO once you have the right ingredients. There are so many alternatives to traditional white (wheat) flour, you'll never miss out. Some of my favorite ingredients to create a crisp on my foods are Parmesan cheese, crushed nuts, almond or soy flour, crushed pork rinds, and, as featured here, textured vegetable protein (TVP). The crispy fried coating on these FOMO Fried Green Tomatoes is so tasty, I don't want any of it to fall off. Since the air fryer method is so gentle on the coating, this recipe turns out perfectly.

2 pounds green tomatoes

1 cup superfine blanched almond flour

1 teaspoon paprika

½ teaspoon salt

¼ teaspoon ground black pepper

3 large eggs

3 tablespoons heavy whipping cream

1 cup textured vegetable protein (TVP)

1 Trim ends off tomatoes and slice into discs ¼"–⅜" thick, cutting through the center axes of tomatoes.

2 Set out two dinner plates and one medium bowl. On one plate, combine flour, paprika, salt, and pepper. In the bowl, whisk together eggs and cream. Spread TVP on remaining plate.

3 Coat both sides of tomato slices first in flour dredge. Then dip in egg wash and shake off extra. Finally, press both sides of each slice into TVP.

4 Arrange coated slices on an air fryer crisper tray, making sure they are not touching. Cook 10 minutes at 400°F, flip, and cook another 10 minutes at the same temperature.

5 Repeat in small batches until done. Serve warm.

Pantry Staples

superfine blanched almond flour, salt, ground black pepper

NET CARBS

5G

SERVES 8

PER SERVING

CALORIES	103
FAT	5G
PROTEIN	7G
SODIUM	99MG
FIBER	3G
CARBOHYDRATES	8G
NET CARBS	5G
SUGAR	5G
SUGAR ALCOHOL	0G

TIME

PREP TIME:	20 MINUTES
COOK TIME:	1 HOUR, 20 MINUTES

TIPS & OPTIONS

Feel free to substitute TVP with an equal amount of ground pork rinds.

Never crowd food inside an air fryer. Otherwise, the circulating heat won't be able to quickly cook the food. The space in between the food is actually *where the magic happens!* I like to think of the air fryer method as built-in portion control.

No air fryer available? Pop them in the oven at 425°F until edges turn golden brown.

Serve these tomatoes with a low-carb dipping sauce of your choice.

Pantry Staples

salt

NET CARBS

4G

SERVES 2

PER SERVING	
CALORIES	265
FAT	26G
PROTEIN	3G
SODIUM	611MG
FIBER	2G
CARBOHYDRATES	6G
NET CARBS	4G
SUGAR	2G
SUGAR ALCOHOL	0G

TIME

PREP TIME:	5 MINUTES
COOK TIME:	18 MINUTES

TIPS & OPTIONS ≫

For variety, I sometimes substitute avocado oil for coconut oil. It adds a little *je ne sais quoi* (translation…I don't really know).

Crunchy broccoli really hits the spot when you're craving tempura. You get all the flavor but none of those pesky bread carbs.

Those without an air fryer can bake this dish at 425°F until edges of broccoli start to brown.

CALL OF DUTY BROCCOLI

My husband (and cookbook coauthor) often asks me if I learned to cook my broccoli in a war zone. It looks quite dark and crispy coming out of the air fryer, you see, like an explosion just went off. I let him think I've burned the batch, knowing full well he'll walk away in disgust without nibbling from my plate. I secretly relish having it all to myself. The crunchy broccoli might look overcooked (that's intentional). It tastes perfectly delicious!

¼ cup coconut oil, melted

½ teaspoon salt

2 cups broccoli florets

1   In a small bowl, whisk oil and salt together until salt dissolves.

2   Dip the top of each floret in the oil mixture and place half the florets on the slotted crisper tray of an air fryer. Spread out to ensure even cooking.

3   Cook at 400°F for 9 minutes in the air fryer, stopping to shake the basket halfway through. Repeat until all broccoli is cooked. Serve immediately.

CABBAGE CRIBBAGE

My husband (and coauthor) created this recipe during a rainstorm. We were out of groceries and neither of us wanted to venture out to the store during a downpour. In a fit of desperation for something "healthy" to eat, we salvaged a *very-sad*-looking head of cabbage from the back of the refrigerator. What to do with it? Surprisingly, after peeling away the browning and limp layers, we solved the riddle. It didn't take but a few minutes to gussy it up with oil and spices. When baked in the oven, Cabbage Cribbage makes an unexpected yet satisfying treat.

> **3 tablespoons unsalted butter, melted**
>
> **¼ teaspoon garlic powder**
>
> **¼ teaspoon salt**
>
> **⅛ teaspoon ground black pepper**
>
> **½ large cabbage, cut through the stem into 4 wedges (cut through the stem so the wedges stay together)**
>
> **1 cup grated Parmesan cheese, divided**

1. Preheat oven to 375°F. Line a baking sheet with parchment paper.

2. In a small bowl, whisk to combine butter, garlic powder, salt, and pepper. Brush mixture onto both cut sides of each cabbage wedge.

3. Sprinkle ¾ cup Parmesan evenly onto both cut sides of each wedge.

4. Bake 40 minutes, flipping wedges halfway through, until they start to brown.

5. Sprinkle with remaining cheese and serve warm.

Pantry Staples

garlic powder, salt, ground black pepper

NET CARBS

9G

SERVES 4

PER SERVING
CALORIES	220
FAT	14G
PROTEIN	9G
SODIUM	625MG
FIBER	4G
CARBOHYDRATES	13G
NET CARBS	9G
SUGAR	5G
SUGAR ALCOHOL	0G

TIME

PREP TIME:	10 MINUTES
COOK TIME:	40 MINUTES

TIPS & OPTIONS

Play around with the spices here when making this as a side dish. I've had great luck using Creole seasoning mix or soy sauce to boost a theme-night meal.

If you're grocery shopping on a tight budget this week, look no further! A head of cabbage is an affordable, low-carb vegetable that feeds a crowd. As an added bonus, it doesn't spoil quickly.

FREEDOM ASPARAGUS FRIES

Pantry Staples

superfine blanched almond flour, baking powder, garlic powder, salt, ground black pepper

NET CARBS

4G

SERVES 6

PER SERVING	
CALORIES	131
FAT	8G
PROTEIN	8G
SODIUM	228MG
FIBER	3G
CARBOHYDRATES	7G
NET CARBS	4G
SUGAR	2G
SUGAR ALCOHOL	0G

TIME

PREP TIME:	10 MINUTES
COOK TIME:	20 MINUTES

TIPS & OPTIONS

Spray asparagus spears with a mist of olive oil prior to baking, and watch the coating transform into a golden McDonald's French fry–style hue. *Now, if I could only match the taste…*

Alternately, you can bake your fries in the oven at 400°F until they become brown.

Dip your "fries" into a thimbleful of mayo. Really!

Fried foods are my weakness, but I won't let French fries become my nemesis! I'm determined to break free and find healthier alternatives. Asparagus fries, made extra crispy in the air fryer, have quickly become my new favorite. Why? Because the "fried" coating turns the most beautiful shade of golden brown. My brain is fooled! This quickie side dish has earned a permanent residency in my DLK kitchen.

> 3 large eggs
> 1 teaspoon heavy whipping cream
> 1 cup superfine blanched almond flour
> 1 cup grated Parmesan cheese
> ¼ teaspoon baking powder
> ¼ teaspoon cayenne pepper
> ¼ teaspoon garlic powder
> ¼ teaspoon salt
> ⅛ teaspoon ground black pepper
> 2 pounds asparagus, trimmed

1 In a shallow 9" × 9" baking dish, whisk together eggs and cream. In a second baking dish of similar size, stir to combine flour, Parmesan, baking powder, cayenne pepper, garlic powder, salt, and black pepper.

2 Coat asparagus spears in egg wash and shake off any extra. Next, roll and press spears into dry mixture until thoroughly coated.

3 Evenly spread half the asparagus on the crisper tray of an air fryer and cook 8–10 minutes at 400°F, turning asparagus over halfway through cooking time.

4 Repeat with remaining half of asparagus until all spears are cooked. Serve warm.

GOLD STAR "SUSHI"

Talk about wow factor.... This dish has it all! It earns five gold stars for presentation, taste, originality, simplicity, *and* net carb count. If that's not enough, putting this dish together is actually a lot of fun (like an edible arts and crafts project). I think you'll agree that Gold Star "Sushi" deserves a spot in the DLK hall of fame. Cue the drumroll, please; I think I've outdone myself.

8 strips thick-cut turkey bacon, cooked but pliable enough to curl into a circle

4 tablespoons full-fat cream cheese, softened, divided

½ medium cucumber, cut into thin, 1"-long sticks

½ medium green bell pepper, cut into thin, 1"-long strips

2 baby carrots, cut into thin, 1"-long sticks

1. Lay bacon strips flat and evenly spread 3 tablespoons cream cheese on top side.

2. Evenly place cucumber, bell pepper, and carrots in a tight, organized manner on top of cream cheese. Only cover the first 4"–5" of each strip, leaving the end bare for overlap. Starting from the vegetable-covered end, tightly roll bacon strips into a sushi-like circle. Secure with remaining 1 tablespoon cream cheese (or a toothpick if the bacon is stubborn).

3. Transfer rolls to a serving plate, placed on their side. Serve immediately.

Pantry Staples

n/a

NET CARBS

3G

SERVES 4

PER SERVING	
CALORIES	274
FAT	20G
PROTEIN	17G
SODIUM	832MG
FIBER	1G
CARBOHYDRATES	4G
NET CARBS	3G
SUGAR	2G
SUGAR ALCOHOL	0G

TIME

PREP TIME:	10 MINUTES
COOK TIME:	0 MINUTES

TIPS & OPTIONS

Sprinkle ½ teaspoon roasted black sesame seeds over your sushi (and platter) to mimic Japanese sushi.

For variety, add pieces of red bell pepper, sprouts, an asparagus tip, or a section of avocado to each roll.

Don't forget the soy sauce!

NET CARBS

7G

SERVES 8

PER SERVING

CALORIES	191
FAT	12G
PROTEIN	10G
SODIUM	378MG
FIBER	3G
CARBOHYDRATES	10G
NET CARBS	7G
SUGAR	3G
SUGAR ALCOHOL	0G

TIME

PREP TIME: 10 MINUTES
COOK TIME: 55 MINUTES

TIPS & OPTIONS ≫

If you're not a fan of Swiss cheese, substitute your family's preference. Cheddar never lets anyone down!

Give your broccoli bake a protein boost by adding leftover protein from last night's dinner. No leftovers? Quickly sauté about 1½ pounds chicken strips in a separate medium skillet and add cooked meat to casserole.

For a bit of color, sprinkle with chopped red bell pepper or paprika prior to baking. This would make for a festive holiday dish, no?

CUT-A-CORNER VEGGIE CASSEROLE

I buy what's convenient and on sale. My vegetables don't have to be fresh—canned or frozen work just as well—especially when baked in a casserole. Cutting corners with ingredients helps me cook healthy meals faster (and stay on track with DLK). I created this casserole after catching a BOGO sale on Swiss cheese. I bought some extra, which I promptly froze to avoid spoiling, thank you very much. With canned mushrooms and frozen broccoli and cauliflower mix, this tasty side dish is easy and economical to make. It's sure to soon become one of your family's favorites as well.

- **1 tablespoon olive oil**
  2 cups drained, sliced canned mushrooms
  1 cup full-fat sour cream
  1½ cups shredded Swiss cheese
- **1 teaspoon garlic powder**
- **½ teaspoon salt**
- **¼ teaspoon ground black pepper**
  8 cups broccoli and cauliflower floret mix

1   Preheat oven to 350°F. Grease a 9" × 12" × 2" baking dish.

2   Heat oil in a large soup pot. Add mushrooms and sauté 5 minutes. Add sour cream, cheese, garlic powder, salt, and pepper and simmer 5 minutes.

3   Add broccoli and cauliflower mixture to a large microwave-safe bowl, then microwave 5 minutes to partially soften.

4   Stir florets into pot with mushroom mixture until coated.

5   Transfer mixture to the prepared baking dish and bake covered 35–40 minutes. Serve warm.

HOT-TO-TROT MUSHROOM SALAD

Once you get past the "creepiness" of mushrooms, they can become your new best friend. Mushrooms aren't just a pizza topping, after all. With only 2g net carbs per 1-cup serving, this overlooked vegetable begins to look pretty sexy! Expand your definition of what a salad looks like. Mushrooms could be the "new lettuce."

> **3 tablespoons apple cider vinegar**
> **1 tablespoon olive oil**
> **½ tablespoon garlic powder**
> **¼ teaspoon salt**
> **⅛ teaspoon ground black pepper**
> **2 pounds portobello mushrooms, chopped into bite-sized pieces**
> **½ cup seeded and thinly sliced red bell pepper**
> **1 tablespoon finely chopped green onion**

1   In a medium mixing bowl, whisk to combine vinegar, oil, garlic powder, salt, and black pepper.

2   Pour vinegar marinade into a 2-gallon resealable bag along with mushrooms and bell pepper. Seal after all the air is squeezed out. Knead the bag until all the vegetables are completely coated with marinade.

3   Let marinate in refrigerator at least 2 hours, preferably overnight.

4   Add contents of bag to a large skillet over medium heat. Cook covered for 15 minutes, stirring regularly.

5   Let cool and serve warm topped with green onion as a garnish.

Pantry Staples

olive oil, garlic powder, salt, ground black pepper

NET CARBS

5G

SERVES 6

PER SERVING

CALORIES	61
FAT	2G
PROTEIN	3G
SODIUM	111MG
FIBER	2G
CARBOHYDRATES	7G
NET CARBS	5G
SUGAR	4G
SUGAR ALCOHOL	0G

TIME

PREP TIME: 15 MINUTES,
PLUS 2 HOURS (OR MORE)
MARINATING TIME
COOK TIME: 15 MINUTES

TIPS & OPTIONS

Mushrooms "bleed" water during the cooking process. At first, expect to see an increased amount of liquid while you sauté the mushrooms.

Sometimes I make this dish on the barbecue. It's easy to bring to a social event! Bring the Ziploc bag of mushroom mixture to a party and transfer it to a makeshift frying pan made of heavy-duty aluminum foil placed directly on the grill over medium heat.

CANOODLING CRAB RANGOONS

NET CARBS

1G

SERVES 10

PER SERVING

CALORIES	96
FAT	7G
PROTEIN	7G
SODIUM	169MG
FIBER	0G
CARBOHYDRATES	1G
NET CARBS	1G
SUGAR	0G
SUGAR ALCOHOL	0G

TIME

PREP TIME:	15 MINUTES
COOK TIME:	25 MINUTES

TIPS & OPTIONS »

Whatever you do, do not buy imitation crab. Fake crab is actually flavored mystery meat made with a combination of assorted minced fish, sugar, starch, and *who knows what else!*

Fresh crab meat is often quite pricey. I buy the more affordable canned crab meat instead (sold next to canned tuna).

No air fryer? Bake rangoons in the oven at 400°F until they reach your desired level of crispiness.

Ordering Chinese food can be tricky on DIRTY, LAZY, KETO. Dishes made with dumplings, noodles, or white rice are an obvious no-go, but what about the rest? Many innocuous-looking Chinese food dishes are laced with sugar. Corn starch added to thicken sauces also hides unwanted carbs. You'll have to make extra careful menu choices and be specific about how you want your food prepared. Even better, stay home and make Chinese food yourself. With this simple Canoodling Crab Rangoons recipe under your belt, you may never order takeout again.

- 5 teaspoons olive oil, divided
- 5 large eggs, divided
- 1 (6-ounce) can crab meat, drained and finely shredded
- 5 tablespoons full-fat cream cheese, softened
- 1 teaspoon onion powder
- ½ teaspoon garlic powder
- ¼ teaspoon salt

1 In a small skillet over medium-high heat, heat 1 teaspoon oil.

2 In a small bowl, beat one egg. Pour egg into skillet, coating entire bottom.

3 Using a spatula, lift the edges of the egg as it becomes firm. Tilt the skillet to allow raw egg to fill in the gaps along the edge of the pan, creating a thin, solid pancake shape. Cook 1 minute, then transfer to a plate. Repeat and make four additional egg pancakes, heating 1 teaspoon oil prior to cooking each egg.

4 Cut egg pancakes evenly into quarters, making twenty egg triangle shapes.

5 In a medium mixing bowl, combine crab, cream cheese, onion powder, garlic powder, and salt.

6 Dollop equal amounts of the crab mixture (about 1 teaspoon each) in the center of the egg triangles. Fold over and pinch to close. Repeat until the mixture is gone.

7 Spread out half the rangoons, without letting them touch, on the crisper tray in an air fryer basket. Bake 9 minutes at 400°F. Repeat with remaining half until all rangoons are "fried." Serve immediately.

NET CARBS

2G

SERVES 8

PER SERVING

CALORIES	132
FAT	11G
PROTEIN	4G
SODIUM	300MG
FIBER	1G
CARBOHYDRATES	3G
NET CARBS	2G
SUGAR	2G
SUGAR ALCOHOL	0G

TIME

PREP TIME: 10 MINUTES
COOK TIME: 20 MINUTES

TIPS & OPTIONS

Ultra-lazy chefs like me might want to know about this sneaky trick: Scoop store-bought creamy dip (e.g., jalapeño, artichoke, or spinach dip) into your freshly cleaned mushroom caps and bake as directed. No one will ever suspect you skipped a few steps!

Mushrooms tend to leak water when heated. Mop up any liquid prior to serving because *that's not pretty.*

SO SATISFYING STUFFED MUSHROOMS

Buying premade stuffed mushroom caps from the deli is one of my guilty pleasures. *Shhh!* For almost the price of the ingredients (at least that's what I tell myself), I can buy a ready-made gourmet platter of appetizers. When I'm feeling inspired to cook (translation: I'm too lazy to make a trip to the store), I make this equally satisfying homemade version.

- ½ teaspoon salt, divided
- **6 ounces full-fat cream cheese, softened**
- **⅓ cup grated Parmesan cheese**
- **¼ teaspoon onion powder**
- **¼ teaspoon dried oregano**
- ¼ teaspoon garlic powder
- ⅛ teaspoon ground black pepper
- **24 medium (width of 1"–2") mushroom caps, cleaned**
- 2 tablespoons olive oil

1 Preheat oven to 390°F. Place a wire rack on a parchment paper–lined baking sheet.

2 In a medium bowl, stir to combine ¼ teaspoon salt, cream cheese, Parmesan, onion powder, oregano, garlic powder, and pepper.

3 Evenly stuff each mushroom cap with cheese mixture.

4 Pour oil into a small bowl. Dip bottoms of each mushroom cap into oil, then sprinkle with remaining ¼ teaspoon salt.

5 Place caps on the wire rack so they are not touching and bake 17–20 minutes until caps soften and cheese mixture starts to brown. Serve warm.

UNWED ONION RINGS

When I'm feeling hormonal (TMI?), I crave salty, fried foods—*preferably dipped in ranch dressing*. In my previous life, those cravings led to serious weight gain! I needed to divorce myself of bad habits and figure out a work-around. With Unwed Onion Rings, I know I can indulge my cravings yet stay on track with my weight loss goals. I love how easy they are to make. I don't need to heat up huge pans of oil, because the fat from the bacon does the "frying" of the onion rings for me. *How easy is that?*

2 large yellow onions, peeled, ends trimmed

1 pound thin-cut no-sugar-added bacon

½ cup Pickle-Tickled Ranch Dressing (see Chapter 5)

1 Preheat oven to 370°F. Line a baking sheet with parchment paper.

2 Cut onions into ½" slices, creating rings. Separate all rings.

3 Wrap large rings with one strip of bacon each. Smaller rings can be wrapped with half strips until all bacon is used.

4 Space rings out on the prepared baking sheet so they are not touching. Cook 15–20 minutes, flipping once, until bacon is crispy.

5 Let cool and serve warm with Pickle-Tickled Ranch Dressing for dipping.

Pantry Staples

n/a

NET CARBS

8G

SERVES 4

PER SERVING	
CALORIES	280
FAT	19G
PROTEIN	15G
SODIUM	977MG
FIBER	1G
CARBOHYDRATES	9G
NET CARBS	8G
SUGAR	4G
SUGAR ALCOHOL	0G

TIME

PREP TIME:	10 MINUTES
COOK TIME:	20 MINUTES

TIPS & OPTIONS

The thinner-sliced bacon is easier to wrap around the onion rings.

Add hot sauce to your ranch dressing dip for a little added zip.

For a quicker cook, impatient chefs can bake these in the air fryer for about 10 minutes (tossing at the midpoint) at 400°F.

FREAKY FRY-DAY GREEN BEANS

When green beans are in season, I can't stop eating them. Learning to cook them in the air fryer has been life changing for me (yes, I do get this excited about food). Gone are the *smushy* steamed beans I've tolerated for decades. There's a new sheriff in town! Move over, Instant Pot®—make room for my new favorite appliance, the air fryer. Crispy, sweet, and made turbo fast, air-fried green beans are here to stay.

> **1 pound fresh green beans, trimmed**
> **2 tablespoons olive oil**
> **½ tablespoon soy sauce**
> **½ teaspoon garlic powder**
> **⅛ teaspoon ground black pepper**
> **1 tablespoon sesame seeds**

1. In a large bowl, use tongs to toss green beans with oil, soy sauce, garlic powder, and pepper.

2. Evenly spread half the beans on the crisper tray of an air fryer and sprinkle with half the sesame seeds. Bake 12 minutes at 400°F, removing the tray to shake the beans halfway through cooking.

3. Transfer cooked beans to a plate and repeat with remaining green beans. Serve warm.

Pantry Staples

olive oil, garlic powder, ground black pepper

NET CARBS

5G

SERVES 4

PER SERVING	
CALORIES	105
FAT	8G
PROTEIN	2G
SODIUM	115MG
FIBER	3G
CARBOHYDRATES	8G
NET CARBS	5G
SUGAR	3G
SUGAR ALCOHOL	0G

TIME

PREP TIME:	10 MINUTES
COOK TIME:	24 MINUTES

TIPS & OPTIONS

For less crispy beans, remove from air fryer at 10-minute mark.

The size of your air fryer determines how much food you can cook at one time. It's important for the food to have room to breathe; avoid overcrowding.

Skip the air fryer method altogether and bake beans at 400°F until they begin to crisp.

CHAPTER 9

MAIN DISHES

When you're new to the DIRTY, LAZY, KETO WOE (way of eating), cooking a main dish is probably the most intimidating. If you're cooking for more than just yourself, you might even be feeling anxious about how your family will react to low-carb cooking. Before you even get started cooking dinner, I'm going to alleviate your concerns and prepare you to handle potential obstacles (aka difficult spouses or children).

First of all, I want you to repeat after me: "Fat tastes delicious!" DIRTY, LAZY, KETO recipes are higher in fat than foods you may have cooked in the past (which is on purpose, remember?). Fat makes healthier foods, like vegetables, taste better. Your lasagna, tacos, and chicken will taste better now *than ever before*. Families are often surprised (and delighted) by the change.

It's also okay to keep things simple at mealtime. In fact, I encourage it! I don't particularly enjoy spending hours cooking in the kitchen either (yes, the irony is not lost here; I'm a cookbook writer, after all).

Instead of overwhelming yourself with gourmet meal planning, build meals around this simple plate concept: **protein + vegetable + fat**.

When it's time to eat, I recommend serving dinner family style. At my house, family members on the eat-o (non-keto) diet can continue to eat high-starch side dishes if they want to. *Gasp!* I don't force my lifestyle on anyone. If a side of rice, pasta, bread, or tortillas helps to keep the peace at dinnertime for those who insist, who am I to argue?

Whether your family is on board or not, remember that your needs are NUMBER ONE. You are worth all of this effort! It takes COURAGE to change your eating habits, and I for one am proud of you. In the long run, your family will be healthier and you will all live better lives. Stick with it. DIRTY, LAZY, KETO WORKS!

ALFREDO FOOLED NOODLES

Can you ever have too much Alfredo sauce in your diet? I think not. I'll top just about anything with this creamy gift from heaven and feel so *satisfied*. I don't feel like I'm on a restrictive "diet" at all. The trick, though, is to enjoy Alfredo sauce with a side of common sense. Use it to make healthy foods taste better (like broccoli, asparagus, or even salmon, for example). This is one of the founding principles behind DIRTY, LAZY, KETO that makes the lifestyle so effective with weight loss.

- 1 tablespoon olive oil
- ⅔ cup sliced mushrooms
- ½ cup heavy whipping cream
- ¼ cup shredded Parmesan cheese
- ¼ teaspoon garlic powder
- ½ teaspoon Italian seasoning
- ⅛ teaspoon salt
- ⅛ teaspoon ground black pepper
- 1 medium zucchini, peeled into zoodles with a julienne peeler

1 Heat oil in a medium skillet over medium heat. Add mushrooms and sauté 4–5 minutes.

2 Add remaining ingredients except zucchini. Simmer 10 minutes while stirring until well blended.

3 Add zoodles to skillet and toss to evenly coat. Cook 5 minutes, stirring often, until tender.

4 Divide onto two dinner plates and serve warm.

Pantry Staples

olive oil, garlic powder, salt, ground black pepper

NET CARBS

7G

SERVES 2

PER SERVING

CALORIES	339
FAT	31G
PROTEIN	7G
SODIUM	401MG
FIBER	1G
CARBOHYDRATES	8G
NET CARBS	7G
SUGAR	5G
SUGAR ALCOHOL	0G

TIME

PREP TIME:	15 MINUTES
COOK TIME:	20 MINUTES

TIPS & OPTIONS

Spice it up by adding a teaspoon of red pepper flakes to the sauce. This will add some grown-up zing *and* a bit of color.

There are many ways to cook zucchini noodles. In lieu of cooking zoodles in a skillet (as directed here), try submerging them in boiling water for only 1 minute. *That's how fast they will cook!* If that method doesn't tickle your fancy, microwave zoodles in a covered microwave-safe dish for only a few minutes.

TIPS & OPTIONS

Add your favorite low-carb produce toppings like shredded lettuce, tomato, jalapeño, avocado, onion, and pickles. Spread your preferred condiments on the bun. Low-carb options include full-fat mayonnaise, no-sugar-added ketchup, and mustard (yellow or spicy).

Want to know my personal favorite way to top the Big Mama Chaffle Burger? With a heaping serving of Pickle-Tickled Ranch Dressing (see Chapter 5). The messier the burger, the better, I say!

BIG MAMA CHAFFLE BURGER

My bottomless freezer stores all sorts of DLK staples. Hidden under numerous value packs of frozen riced cauliflower you'll find towers of mysterious frozen "burger" patties. I keep a variety of styles on hand—beef, turkey, chicken, and salmon. I'm ready to barbecue! (Exactly what? I'd have to guess.) Provided I can chip one patty off the tower of frozen meat (the packaged burgers always seem to "glue" together, right?), I can quickly grill up a Big Mama Chaffle Burger tonight.

Chaffle Bun (2 halves)

1 cup shredded Cheddar cheese

2 medium eggs, beaten

½ teaspoon heavy whipping cream

½ teaspoon garlic powder

⅛ teaspoon ground black pepper

Burger and Toppings

1 (85% lean) beef burger patty

1 (1-ounce) deli slice pepper jack cheese

1 Lightly spray a waffle maker with nonstick cooking spray and preheat.

2 In a medium bowl, mix all Chaffle Bun ingredients. Evenly divide the mixture between two squares in waffle maker and cook 3 minutes.

3 In a small skillet over medium heat, cook patty 5–7 minutes on each side. Top with slice of cheese (after the flip) while still in the skillet.

4 Insert cheeseburger between two chaffles (like a bun) and serve warm.

SHORTCUT SAUSAGE SKILLET

Pantry Staples

olive oil, garlic powder, salt, ground black pepper

NET CARBS

7G

SERVES 4

PER SERVING

CALORIES	418
FAT	30G
PROTEIN	26G
SODIUM	1,178MG
FIBER	3G
CARBOHYDRATES	10G
NET CARBS	7G
SUGAR	4G
SUGAR ALCOHOL	0G

TIME

PREP TIME:	10 MINUTES
COOK TIME:	24 MINUTES

TIPS & OPTIONS ⟫

One of my favorite precooked, low-carb sausage brands is Aidells. For this recipe, I often use Aidells Italian Style Smoked Chicken Sausage with Mozzarella Cheese. It has 1g net carbs per 1-link (85g) serving.

I love making dinners that fool my guests into thinking I labored away over a hot stove all day. I often take hidden shortcuts with ingredients when I can. Take this Shortcut Sausage Skillet, for example. Buying precooked sausages at the supermarket cuts down on the recipe steps. Shortcuts allow me to quickly assemble mouthwatering, gourmet meals in just minutes.

- 2 tablespoons olive oil
- 1 (12-ounce) package precooked sausage, sliced
- ½ medium yellow onion, peeled and chopped
- 1 medium green bell pepper, seeded and chopped
- 4 cups shredded cabbage
- ¼ teaspoon garlic powder
- ¼ teaspoon salt
- ⅛ teaspoon ground black pepper
- 2 cups shredded whole milk mozzarella cheese

1. Heat oil in a large cast iron skillet over medium heat. Add sausage and onion and cook 5 minutes to brown while stirring.

2. Stir in remaining ingredients except cheese. Reduce heat to simmer and cook 15 minutes while covered, stirring regularly.

3. Preheat broiler on high.

4. Remove the skillet from the heat and take off the lid. Evenly top the mixture in the skillet with cheese. Place under the broiler 2–4 minutes until cheese is melted and begins to brown.

5. Remove from broiler and let cool slightly. Serve warm.

MANLY MAN STROGANOFF

Remember the TV dinners of yesteryear? The Hungry-Man steak meal was my all-time favorite (for its large portions, obviously). Hearty and filling dinners are not a thing of the past with DLK. Put some hair on your chest with these hefty portions of comfort food. *No wimpy salad tonight!* Shut down potential complaints from keto naysayers in your family by making mouthwatering stroganoff for dinner.

- 1 tablespoon olive oil
  1½ pounds boneless top sirloin, cut into ¼" strips
  ½ medium yellow onion, peeled and chopped
  1 pound mushrooms, sliced
- ¼ teaspoon garlic powder
- ¼ teaspoon salt
- ⅛ teaspoon ground black pepper
  ½ cup full-fat sour cream
- 1 cup vegetable broth

1 Heat oil in a medium saucepan over medium heat. Add sirloin, onion, mushrooms, garlic powder, salt, and pepper and toss to combine. Cook 15 minutes, stirring regularly.

2 Stir in sour cream and broth and cook covered another 10 minutes, stirring regularly.

3 Serve warm.

Pantry Staples

olive oil, garlic powder, salt, ground black pepper, vegetable broth

NET CARBS

6G

SERVES 4

PER SERVING

CALORIES	364
FAT	17G
PROTEIN	43G
SODIUM	449MG
FIBER	1G
CARBOHYDRATES	7G
NET CARBS	6G
SUGAR	4G
SUGAR ALCOHOL	0G

TIME

PREP TIME:	15 MINUTES
COOK TIME:	25 MINUTES

TIPS & OPTIONS

Substitute any other type of broth (beef, chicken, and so on) for the vegetable broth. You are mixing it with steak, after all.

A thick and bold meal like stroganoff screams to be served with *taters*, right? Do your carb count one better and whip up a batch of faux mashed potatoes (steamed cauliflower whipped into a smooth frenzy with butter, sour cream, garlic, and plenty of salt).

CRASH COURSE CARNITAS

Let's be honest: When you're thinking about what to make for dinner, the recipes with the shortest number of ingredients tend to jump out at you first. They might seem less intimidating—even goof-proof! But a short ingredient list doesn't have to mean a sacrifice in flavor. Less can be more. Take this Crash Course Carnitas recipe, for example. Even a novice can pull this one together! This straightforward recipe makes a delicious, hearty meal that the entire family will enjoy.

> 3 pounds boneless pork shoulder roast, trimmed
>
> 3 medium limes, cut in half
>
> 2 tablespoons taco powder seasoning mix
>
> 1 teaspoon garlic powder
>
> 1 teaspoon salt
>
> ½ teaspoon ground black pepper
>
> 1 medium white onion, peeled and quartered
>
> 2 tablespoons chopped fresh cilantro

1 Place roast in a slow cooker. Squeeze juice from limes to coat all sides of roast. Cut limes into rounds and set aside.

2 In a small bowl, combine taco seasoning, garlic powder, salt, and pepper. Whisk to blend. Sprinkle seasoning on all sides of roast. Place onion and lime rounds on top of roast.

3 Cook on high 4–5 hours until meat is cooked through.

4 Preheat broiler. Line a baking sheet with foil and spray with nonstick cooking spray.

5 Let roast cool slightly, then remove roast and onions to a plate to drain, discarding the lime peels. Shred meat and onions using two forks. Spread shredded mixture evenly on the prepared baking sheet.

6 Place under broiler until meat begins to crisp, 2–3 minutes.

7 Top with sprinkled cilantro. Serve.

Pantry Staples

garlic powder, salt, ground black pepper

NET CARBS

4G

SERVES 6

PER SERVING

CALORIES	471
FAT	29G
PROTEIN	39G
SODIUM	705MG
FIBER	1G
CARBOHYDRATES	5G
NET CARBS	4G
SUGAR	1G
SUGAR ALCOHOL	0G

TIME

PREP TIME:	15 MINUTES
COOK TIME:	5 HOURS, 3 MINUTES

TIPS & OPTIONS

Enjoy carnitas in a variety of DLK ways—solo, on lettuce wraps, in a low-carb tortilla, or on top of a salad. Family members on the eat-o (non-keto) diet might enjoy making tacos with corn tortillas. The key to keeping the peace, in my opinion, is serving meals like this family style.

If you're without a slow cooker, bake covered carnitas in the oven at 275°F until internal temperature reaches 160°F (medium) or 170°F (well done).

COMPLETE CUBANO PORK WRAPS

Pantry Staples

olive oil, garlic powder, salt, ground black pepper

NET CARBS

3G

SERVES 2

PER SERVING

CALORIES	589
FAT	35G
PROTEIN	62G
SODIUM	1,251MG
FIBER	2G
CARBOHYDRATES	5G
NET CARBS	3G
SUGAR	2G
SUGAR ALCOHOL	0G

TIME

PREP TIME: 10 MINUTES, PLUS 30 MINUTES (OR MORE) MARINATING TIME

COOK TIME: 15 MINUTES

TIPS & OPTIONS ≫

Just like you would smear on bread, add full-fat mayonnaise and yellow mustard to your lettuce wrap. *A little dab will do ya.*

Substitute Swiss cheese for the provolone, if you prefer.

Beef up your Cuban (sorry, should I say "pork up"?) by adding another layer of warm deli ham slices.

I first learned to cook pork in my slow cooker. Other than forgetting to plug it in (which I have done), I found this method quite dependable! It was hard for me to try a new way, but I've learned that frying meat on the stovetop can be just as forgiving. The trick to making melt-in-your-mouth pork, I've discovered, is the marinade. It pulls it all together and provides the magnificent flavor and tenderness.

+ **3 tablespoons olive oil, divided**

1 tablespoon 100% lime juice

+ **½ teaspoon garlic powder**

+ **¼ teaspoon salt**

+ **⅛ teaspoon ground black pepper**

1 pound boneless pork chops, thinly sliced into bite-sized pieces

4 medium leaves romaine lettuce

2 (1-ounce) deli slices provolone cheese, halved

1 large dill pickle, thinly sliced

1   In a large bowl, whisk together 2 tablespoons oil, lime juice, garlic powder, salt, and pepper. Stir in pork until all pieces are completely coated. Cover and refrigerate at least 30 minutes, preferably 2 hours.

2   In a medium skillet over medium heat, heat remaining 1 tablespoon oil.

3   Transfer pork mixture and marinade to the skillet and cook covered 15 minutes while stirring regularly.

4   Arrange two romaine leaves on each of two dinner plates and evenly fill with cooked meat mixture.

5   Top each with half slice provolone and pickles. Serve immediately.

HIGHBROW HOT DIGGITY DOGS

Does DLK have to be fancy? Not at my house. Grinding away in the kitchen all day doesn't necessarily make food taste better. Oftentimes, the simplest ingredients, assembled in only a couple of steps, wins over the crowd. Take hot dogs, for example. With a quick "slit, spread, and stuff," this inexpensive dinner will soon become a familiar family favorite.

> 2 all-beef hot dogs
>
> 1 (1-ounce) deli slice Cheddar cheese, cut into strips ¼" wide
>
> ½ tablespoon seeded and diced jalapeño
>
> 4 strips thin-cut no-sugar-added bacon
>
> ⅛ teaspoon garlic powder
>
> ⅛ teaspoon ground black pepper

1 Preheat oven to 380°F. Place a wire rack on a parchment paper–lined baking sheet.

2 Lay hot dogs on the wire rack of the prepared baking sheet. Slice lengthwise to make a pocket, leaving a ½" uncut buffer at each end, creating a "boat" to stuff with fillings.

3 Insert even amounts cheese and jalapeño into each hot dog. Wrap stuffed hot dogs with 2 strips bacon each in a spiral pattern. Wrap in opposing directions to create a uniform "jacket" to hold in the melted cheese.

4 Arrange on the wire rack with the slit side of the dog facing up. Sprinkle with garlic powder and black pepper.

5 Cook 20–25 minutes until bacon is crispy. Cover with foil when starting to brown. Serve warm.

Pantry Staples

garlic powder, ground black pepper

NET CARBS

2G

SERVES 2

PER SERVING

CALORIES	313
FAT	25G
PROTEIN	16G
SODIUM	939MG
FIBER	0G
CARBOHYDRATES	2G
NET CARBS	2G
SUGAR	1G
SUGAR ALCOHOL	0G

TIME

PREP TIME:	10 MINUTES
COOK TIME:	25 MINUTES

TIPS & OPTIONS

Get creative with added fillings. The bacon wrap will hold it all together, so *get to stuffin'*.

If hot dogs don't hold a place in your heart, substitute a precooked "grown-up" sausage (like Aidells).

Double or quadruple this recipe and reheat to enjoy later. Quickly microwave 30–45 seconds to enjoy these scrumptious little flavor rockets as an afternoon snack.

NET CARBS

6G

SERVES 4

PER SERVING	
CALORIES	252
FAT	13G
PROTEIN	21G
SODIUM	363MG
FIBER	2G
CARBOHYDRATES	8G
NET CARBS	6G
SUGAR	2G
SUGAR ALCOHOL	0G

TIME

PREP TIME:	10 MINUTES
COOK TIME:	20 MINUTES

TIPS & OPTIONS

Additional low-carb toppings are welcome! Add to your heart's desire: jalapeño, pickle, avocado, onion, or grilled mushrooms.

No burger is complete without condiments such as no-sugar-added ketchup, full-fat mayonnaise, or mustard.

SLIP 'N' SLIDE QUESO BURGERS

Romaine boats are surprisingly sturdy. Even when filled to the brim with cheesy queso, they still won't leak or fall apart! Perhaps due to novelty (or crunch), my kids actually prefer romaine leaves over hamburger buns. I make it a point to use them for all sorts of meals—sandwiches, tacos, wraps. No matter what your age, you'll have fun filling and eating this appetizing cheeseburger boat.

4 (85% lean) beef burger patties
1 (4-ounce) can mild green chilies, drained and chopped
½ cup queso
4 large leaves romaine lettuce
1 large beefsteak tomato, diced

1   In a large skillet over medium heat, cook all patties 5–7 minutes on each side. Using a spatula, cut patties in half. Remove from pan and set aside.

2   Drain fat from skillet, add chilies, and sauté 3–5 minutes.

3   In a small microwave-safe glass bowl, microwave queso 1 minute. Stir.

4   Lay romaine leaves on four dinner plates and fill each with equal amounts hamburger, chilies, queso, and tomato. Serve warm.

ONE MINUTE MAN ENCHILADAS

Pantry Staples

n/a

NET CARBS

7G

SERVES 2

PER SERVING

CALORIES	252
FAT	10G
PROTEIN	30G
SODIUM	965MG
FIBER	3G
CARBOHYDRATES	10G
NET CARBS	7G
SUGAR	6G
SUGAR ALCOHOL	0G

TIME

PREP TIME: 20 MINUTES
COOK TIME: 1 MINUTE

TIPS & OPTIONS ⟫

Enjoy a dollop of full-fat sour cream, chopped green onion, or salsa on top of your "enchiladas."

Instead of cabbage, substitute finely shredded lettuce.

Go traditional with your enchilada if you wish: Roll up the meat in a low-carb tortilla, sprinkle with cheese, and serve with a side of lettuce. I recommend you give La Tortilla Factory brand a try (only 6g of net carbs per tortilla). Another crowd favorite is made by Mission Carb Balance with 3g net carbs per tortilla.

Like a little kick? Sprinkle fresh shredded radish on top of your dish. *Olé!*

Low-carb cooking isn't rocket science and shouldn't take all day. Leftovers, a microwave, and a little creativity might be all you need to make a tasty meal! My One Minute Man Enchiladas recipe is proof. Mexican "casseroles" don't need to take hours and hours of prep time. You'll take one bite and say to yourself, "Why didn't I think of doing this sooner?!"

2 cups finely shredded cabbage

1 cup shredded rotisserie chicken breast

½ cup red enchilada sauce

½ cup shredded Monterey jack cheese

1 tablespoon sliced black olives

1 Spread shredded cabbage evenly on two dinner plates.

2 In a medium microwave-safe bowl, combine chicken and enchilada sauce. Microwave 1 minute, stopping halfway through to stir. Evenly divide mixture onto each bed of cabbage.

3 Top each with equal amounts cheese and olives. Serve warm.

PARTY POOPER PRAWNS

To save prep time in the kitchen (and also prevent nightmares), I make it a habit to always buy pre-cleaned shrimp. Do you know what's inside that little black stripe along the back of raw shrimp? I'll give you a hint. It might have to do with the name of this dish. *Maybe you don't want to know.* Do yourself a favor—especially when prepping food for party guests. Cut corners like I did here to make DLK food prep as simple and carefree as possible. Then you can go back to enjoying the party!

1 pound thin-cut turkey bacon, halved to make short strips

2 pounds colossal (16–22 per pound) prawns, peeled and deveined

½ tablespoon water

½ teaspoon garlic powder

½ teaspoon salt

¼ teaspoon ground black pepper

1 Preheat oven to 375°F. Line a baking sheet with parchment paper.

2 Spread bacon out on prepared baking sheet with no overlapping. Bake 8 minutes.

3 Add prawns and water to a large mixing bowl and stir. Top with remaining ingredients and stir to coat.

4 Wrap each seasoned prawn with 1 bacon half and secure with a toothpick. Place on baking sheet so that none of them are touching.

5 Bake 10–15 minutes, turning halfway through. The prawns will be pink when cooked. Serve warm.

Pantry Staples

garlic powder, salt, ground black pepper

NET CARBS

2G

SERVES 8

PER SERVING

CALORIES	209
FAT	7G
PROTEIN	32G
SODIUM	894MG
FIBER	0G
CARBOHYDRATES	2G
NET CARBS	2G
SUGAR	1G
SUGAR ALCOHOL	0G

TIME

PREP TIME:	10 MINUTES
COOK TIME:	23 MINUTES

TIPS & OPTIONS

I make it a point to serve appetizers like these using decorative toothpicks. You know the ones with the shiny tassels on the ends? It only takes one person biting into a sharp toothpick before you, too, will decide to upgrade to the *expensive* (more noticeable) toothpicks. Safety first!

ORANGE CRUSH CHICKEN

When it comes to losing weight, I'm willing to make a lot of sacrifices. I'll exercise in the pouring rain, bring my own snacks on airplanes, even turn down mystery dishes if I don't know what's inside them. But there is one thing I refuse to compromise on…my diet soda! A girl has to draw the line somewhere, and for me that boundary comes in a delicious orange can. My favorite diet soda isn't just a drink. Tonight, it makes a *winner, winner, chicken dinner*!

> 1 pound boneless, skinless chicken thighs
>
> ½ medium white onion, peeled and sliced into wedges
>
> ¼ cup no-sugar-added ketchup
>
> 12 ounces Diet Orange Crush soda
>
> ⅓ cup 0g net carbs sweetener
>
> 2 cups chopped (1" chunks) red and green bell pepper

1   Add all ingredients except bell peppers to a slow cooker and stir to blend. Cook on high 2 hours, 30 minutes.

2   Add bell peppers to slow cooker. Continue cooking 30 minutes on high.

3   Let cool and evenly divide into two bowls. Serve warm.

Pantry Staples

0g net carbs sweetener

NET CARBS

10G

SERVES 2

PER SERVING	
CALORIES	379
FAT	14G
PROTEIN	41G
SODIUM	502MG
FIBER	3G
CARBOHYDRATES	29G
NET CARBS	10G
SUGAR	9G
SUGAR ALCOHOL	16G

TIME

PREP TIME:	10 MINUTES
COOK TIME:	3 HOURS

TIPS & OPTIONS

Expect this dish to be a little *soupy*. To help "mop up" the delicious orange sauce, I serve this sweet dish with a side of plain steamed cauliflower rice.

Folks without a slow cooker can easily modify this recipe on the stovetop using a large covered stockpot. Bring ingredients to a boil, then simmer, covered, until internal temperature of chicken reaches 165°F.

Substitute any color bell pepper here. Note the wide difference in carb count among the colors: red 12g, yellow/orange 8g, and green 4g net carbs per 1-cup serving.

0g net carbs sweetener, garlic powder

NET CARBS

1G

SERVES 6

PER SERVING

CALORIES	208
FAT	16G
PROTEIN	14G
SODIUM	961MG
FIBER	0G
CARBOHYDRATES	3G
NET CARBS	1G
SUGAR	1G
SUGAR ALCOHOL	2G

TIME

PREP TIME: 15 MINUTES
COOK TIME: 15 MINUTES

TIPS & OPTIONS »

Technically, the ham is already cooked, so we are just warming it up and seasoning it here. I wouldn't mention that to anyone, though. This dish looks so impressive, everyone will be telling you to sit down while they offer to do the dishes.

Instead of using a pressure cooker, feel free to warm up your glazed ham in the oven at 325°F until internal temperature of meat reaches 145°F.

I like to make a little extra glaze and serve it in a small bowl with a spoon alongside the ham in the buffet line.

HONEY MUSTARD DAMN HAM

Of the many part-time jobs I had putting myself through school, one of the most memorable (and short-lived) was my time working at the Honey Baked Ham store. You wouldn't believe the lines! I learned people don't play around when it comes to their Christmas dinner. They want their damn ham, and they want it *now*. Personally, I'd rather stay home and make my own damn ham. So, I did.

> 1 (2-pound) ham, unsweetened
> ½ cup full-fat mayonnaise
> 1½ tablespoons yellow mustard
> 1 tablespoon apple cider vinegar
> 2 tablespoons 0g net carbs sweetener
> ½ teaspoon garlic powder
> ¼ teaspoon paprika
> 1 cup water

1 Center ham on a large piece of heavy duty foil that is large enough to wrap completely around ham. Fold up sides of foil so it can retain the glaze, like a big foil bowl.

2 In a medium bowl, stir to combine all remaining ingredients except water until sweetener dissolves.

3 Pour mustard mixture over ham, then use a basting brush to cover the entire ham. Fold the foil over the top of the ham.

4 Add water to an Instant Pot® and place ham (with foil wrap) on a trivet. Secure the lid, close the release, and cook 15 minutes on high pressure.

5 Release pressure and unlock lid.

6 Remove ham to a large plate without foil. Slice and serve warm.

PHONY PHILLY CHEESESTEAK

This classic American sandwich is DLK from the get-go—that is, except for the bread. The "insides" are already low-carb compliant. If steak doesn't tickle your fancy, substitute grilled chicken or portobello mushroom. Use my simple Flatbread substitution and you're ready to make lunch.

Pantry Staples
superfine blanched almond flour, baking powder, salt, ground black pepper, garlic powder

NET CARBS
9G

SERVES 2

PER SERVING	
CALORIES	981
FAT	68G
PROTEIN	64G
SODIUM	1,336MG
FIBER	7G
CARBOHYDRATES	16G
NET CARBS	9G
SUGAR	5G
SUGAR ALCOHOL	0G

TIME
PREP TIME:	10 MINUTES
COOK TIME:	29 MINUTES

Flatbread
- 2 ounces full-fat cream cheese, softened
- 1¼ cups shredded whole milk mozzarella cheese
- 1 large egg, beaten
- 1 cup superfine blanched almond flour
- 1 teaspoon baking powder
- ⅛ teaspoon salt

Cheesesteak
- 8 ounces flank steak, cut into ¼" strips
- 1 tablespoon water
- 1 cup frozen bell pepper and onion blend
- ⅛ teaspoon ground black pepper
- ¼ teaspoon garlic powder
- ⅛ teaspoon salt
- ½ cup shredded whole milk mozzarella cheese

1 Preheat oven to 400°F. Line a baking sheet with parchment paper.

2 Make the Flatbread. To a large microwave-safe bowl, add cream cheese and mozzarella. Microwave 30 seconds. Stir, then microwave again 30 seconds.

3 Mix in eggs, flour, baking powder, and salt until combined and dough forms. Evenly divide dough in two and flatten each portion into a circular shape on the prepared baking sheet until thickness is ¼"–½".

4 Bake 10–13 minutes until firm and starting to brown. Set aside to cool.

5 Next, make the Cheesesteak. To a medium nonstick skillet over medium heat, add all ingredients except mozzarella. Cook 10–15 minutes while stirring.

6 When Flatbreads are cool, lay each on a dinner plate.

7 Top each evenly with steak mixture. Evenly top with mozzarella. Serve warm.

TIPS & OPTIONS

Frozen vegetable blends (like the bell pepper and onion mix used here) are a great time saver. The prep work has been done for you! No cleaning or cutting vegetables tonight, my friend. Take advantage of every loophole when cooking.

Make extra servings of Flatbread (and freeze if you'd like) to enjoy later with the Yippee Chicken Gyros recipe (see recipe in this chapter).

Pantry Staples

salt, ground black pepper, garlic powder

NET CARBS

4G

SERVES 2

PER SERVING

CALORIES	809
FAT	49G
PROTEIN	73G
SODIUM	1,237MG
FIBER	0G
CARBOHYDRATES	4G
NET CARBS	4G
SUGAR	1G
SUGAR ALCOHOL	0G

TIME

PREP TIME:	10 MINUTES
COOK TIME:	14 MINUTES

TIPS & OPTIONS ≫

Double or triple this Chaffle recipe and pop extras into the freezer for future use—for example, when you make the Big Mama Chaffle Burger (see recipe in this chapter). They store so nicely in a large Ziploc bag! Reheat frozen Chaffles on a microwave-safe plate for 1 minute or pop them in the toaster when you're ready to enjoy.

No air fryer? Oven bake chicken at 400°F until internal temperature reaches 165°F.

Fans of buttermilk fried chicken in corn flakes will crow over my DLK version. Ground pork rinds (from a food processor) make an uncanny substitute! After a lot of trial and error (you're welcome, by the way), I learned that cooking fried chicken in the air fryer is the most effective method for keeping the "fried" crust intact. That's really the only part that matters, right?

Fried Chicken

- ⅛ teaspoon salt
- ⅛ teaspoon ground black pepper
- ⅛ teaspoon garlic powder
  2 medium eggs
  1 cup ground pork rinds
  2 (4.2-ounce) boneless, skinless chicken breasts

Chaffles

  2 cups shredded Cheddar cheese
  4 medium eggs, beaten
  1 teaspoon heavy whipping cream
- 1 teaspoon garlic powder
- ¼ teaspoon ground black pepper

1 Make the Fried Chicken. On a dinner plate, combine salt, black pepper, and garlic powder. Crack eggs into a medium bowl and beat. Spread pork rinds on a separate dinner plate.

2 First, lightly coat both sides of chicken with spices, then dip both sides into the egg wash and shake off any excess. Next, press both sides of each breast into pork rinds and place into an air fryer on the crisper tray so that the breasts are not touching.

3 Cook in air fryer at 400°F for 8 minutes until internal temperature reaches 165°F. Set aside.

4 Next, make the Chaffles. Lightly spray a waffle maker with nonstick cooking spray and preheat.

5 In a medium bowl, mix all Chaffle ingredients. Fill four waffle forms with equal amounts batter and cook 3 minutes. Repeat if necessary, until all batter is used.

6 Divide Chaffles onto two plates and place a chicken breast on top. Serve warm.

olive oil, garlic powder, salt, ground black pepper

NET CARBS

4G

SERVES 6

PER SERVING

CALORIES	338
FAT	22G
PROTEIN	26G
SODIUM	550MG
FIBER	1G
CARBOHYDRATES	5G
NET CARBS	4G
SUGAR	3G
SUGAR ALCOHOL	0G

TIME

PREP TIME:	15 MINUTES
COOK TIME:	42 MINUTES

TIPS & OPTIONS 〉〉

Semi-frozen chicken breasts are much easier (and less slippery) to cut. Safety first!

Keep a close eye on your soup pot. Be sure to frequently stir the zucchini and cheese mixture or else risk a crusty brown burn at the bottom of your pot.

SURPRISING SQUASH STEW

The process of becoming a "healthy eater" doesn't happen overnight. Be patient with yourself (especially when it comes to eating more vegetables). Don't assume you're going to wake up one day craving celery—*ain't gonna happen!* On the contrary, you might have to take extraordinary measures in the kitchen to make vegetables taste better on your palate. Get creative adding different spices. Cover them with delicious fats if you have to. Just like I did here with my Surprising Squash Stew recipe, sometimes you have to become innovative to make healthy eating tolerable.

- 1 tablespoon olive oil
  1 pound boneless, skinless chicken breasts, cut into ½"–¾" cubes
- ½ teaspoon garlic powder
  3 medium zucchini, sliced into ¼" half circles
- ½ teaspoon salt
- ⅛ teaspoon ground black pepper
  ½ cup heavy whipping cream
  2 ounces full-fat cream cheese, softened
  6 ounces shredded Cheddar cheese

1 Heat oil in a large soup pot over medium heat. Add chicken and garlic powder and cook 12 minutes while stirring regularly.

2 Reduce heat to low and add remaining ingredients.

3 Cook covered 30 minutes until all cheeses are melted, stirring regularly. Serve warm.

BUFFET LINE BUTTER CHICKEN

When I was pregnant with my son, I craved Indian food constantly. There is just something about it! I couldn't go to the local buffet every day (that would be embarrassing) so I figured out how to make it at home. Over the years, I've played around with many versions of this aromatic dish, but this recipe is the most manageable when it comes to a short list of ingredients and limited cook time required. As you know, *cravings can't wait!*

1 pound boneless, skinless chicken breasts, cut into 1" cubes
2 tablespoons olive oil, divided
2 tablespoons garam masala
2 teaspoons grated fresh ginger
2 teaspoons garlic powder
⅛ teaspoon salt
⅛ teaspoon ground black pepper
1½ cups vegetable broth
¼ cup 100% tomato sauce
¼ cup heavy whipping cream

1   Add chicken and 1 tablespoon oil to a large (2-gallon) resealable bag. Squeeze air out of bag and seal. Knead bag until all chicken is coated. Add garam masala, ginger, garlic powder, salt, and pepper to bag and seal as before. Knead bag again until all chicken is coated. Let marinate in refrigerator at least 1 hour, preferably overnight.

2   In a large skillet over medium heat, heat remaining 1 tablespoon oil. Add chicken and marinade and sauté 5 minutes while stirring.

3   Stir in broth and cook 15 minutes, stirring regularly. Stir in tomato sauce and cream and simmer 3–5 minutes until thickened to desired consistency.

4   Serve warm over your favorite naan or rice substitute.

Pantry Staples

olive oil, garlic powder, salt, ground black pepper, vegetable broth

NET CARBS

5G

SERVES 4

PER SERVING

CALORIES	261
FAT	15G
PROTEIN	27G
SODIUM	641MG
FIBER	0G
CARBOHYDRATES	5G
NET CARBS	5G
SUGAR	2G
SUGAR ALCOHOL	0G

TIME

PREP TIME: 15 MINUTES, PLUS 1 HOUR (OR MORE) MARINATING TIME
COOK TIME: 25 MINUTES

◀◀ TIPS & OPTIONS

Indian-style basmati rice is so 1980s. In its place, might I suggest a side of cauliflower rice? If you prefer something lighter, a green salad, a bed of shredded cabbage, or sliced cucumbers go nicely with hot Buffet Line Butter Chicken poured over the top.

SIMPLE SALAMI SKEWERS

Simple Salami Skewers make a beautiful presentation on the plate. Food served on a stick looks fancy (and is more fun to eat). I serve these in a variety of ways: on top of a bed of shredded cabbage (like a salad), with a side of steaming-hot cauliflower rice (for dinner), or on a platter as an appetizer for parties. Personally, I love keto snacks I can eat with my fingers. Simple Salami Skewers are so delicious and easy to make, even your kids (or picky spouse) will gobble them up!

1 (7-ounce) package large (approximately 3"-diameter) salami slices

½ pound boneless, skinless chicken breasts, cut into ½" cubes

1 cup cubed (¼" cubes) Monterey jack cheese

¼ cup drained and diced sun-dried tomatoes packed in oil

¼ cup fresh basil leaves

1. Preheat oven to 420°F. Line a baking sheet with foil and lightly spray with nonstick cooking spray.

2. Lay salami slices on the prepared baking sheet and top each with equal amounts (in order) of chicken, cheese, tomato, then basil.

3. Fold salami around ingredients (keeping cheese centered) and poke a skewer through the midsection to keep it secure. Thread equal amounts folded salami onto six skewers, with ¼" space between each salami so they are not touching.

4. Arrange skewers on the baking sheet spaced 1" apart and bake 10 minutes. Serve immediately.

Pantry Staples

n/a

NET CARBS

2G

SERVES 6

PER SERVING

CALORIES	254
FAT	17G
PROTEIN	23G
SODIUM	799MG
FIBER	0G
CARBOHYDRATES	2G
NET CARBS	2G
SUGAR	0G
SUGAR ALCOHOL	0G

TIME

PREP TIME:	15 MINUTES
COOK TIME:	10 MINUTES

« TIPS & OPTIONS

Cut basil into attractive ribbons using this simple trick: Stack several leaves on top of one another and roll them into a tight tube. Use a sharp knife to slice the tube into ¼" sections and unroll. Voilà!

Expect the cheese to melt and run out of the salami while baking. I consider this a bonus freebie snack to break off and nibble on before serving.

olive oil, garlic powder, ground black pepper

NET CARBS

10G

SERVES 4

PER SERVING

CALORIES	957
FAT	74G
PROTEIN	48G
SODIUM	1,458MG
FIBER	6G
CARBOHYDRATES	16G
NET CARBS	10G
SUGAR	5G
SUGAR ALCOHOL	0G

TIME

PREP TIME:	15 MINUTES
COOK TIME:	15 MINUTES

TIPS & OPTIONS 》》

In lieu of making freshly baked Flatbread, take a store-bought shortcut. Warm up a low-carb sandwich thin such as Outer Aisle Plantpower Sandwich Thins, which have 2g net carbs per 1-slice (32g) serving.

Need a little support? Wrap your folded-over gyros with aluminum foil. Now it's not as messy to eat.

YIPPEE CHICKEN GYROS

The Greeks really know how to "do keto," in my opinion. I, for one, could eat tzatziki sauce over rotisserie gyro meat, cucumbers, tomatoes, and olives every day for the rest of my life and die a happy camper. The trick to making delicious Greek food (at least at my house) is to add the right blend of spices to each dish. Achieving the right balance can be tricky. That's why I rely on a Greek seasoning blend to do the work for me.

- **1 tablespoon olive oil**
- **4 (3-ounce) boneless, skinless chicken thighs, cut into ½" strips**
- **¼ teaspoon garlic powder**
- **⅛ teaspoon ground black pepper**
- **4 pieces low-carb Flatbread (double the Phony Philly Cheesesteak recipe in this chapter)**
- **½ cup full-fat sour cream**
- **1 teaspoon Greek seasoning**
- **1½ cups Pedestrian Mediterranean Salad (see Chapter 5)**

1   In a medium saucepan over medium heat, heat oil. Add chicken, garlic powder, and pepper. Cook 12–15 minutes, stirring regularly.

2   Set out four plates with a Flatbread on each.

3   In a small bowl, combine sour cream and Greek seasoning.

4   Divide chicken evenly on Flatbreads. Top evenly with equal amounts Pedestrian Mediterranean Salad and sour cream mixture.

5   Serve immediately. Eat gyro folded over as you would a taco.

NO TRICK TRI-TIP

For years I struggled with preparing roasted meat. I tended to serve it raw or coated in char. My loving husband never complained once. He assured me, "That's what takeout is for, honey." *What a sweetie.* It wasn't until I played around with my old cooking thermometer that I figured out what the real problem was with my meat-cooking mojo. The internal "guts" of my thermometer were fried, and I was getting bogus temperature readings! Don't ever give up on your cooking skills, friends. Like me, your lack of skill might not be your fault in the first place (blame technical difficulties).

+ **1 tablespoon olive oil**

3 tablespoons steak seasoning

1 (2½-pound) tri-tip roast

+ **1 cup vegetable broth**

2 cups whole mushrooms

2 cups whole radishes

1 Heat oil in an Instant Pot® on Sauté mode.

2 Spread steak seasoning on a large plate and press roast into it to coat both sides.

3 Add roast to the Instant Pot® and sauté each side 2 minutes.

4 Remove roast and add the trivet to the Instant Pot®. Add broth and return roast to Instant Pot®. Top with mushrooms and radishes.

5 Secure the lid and close the pressure release. Pressure cook on high for 25 minutes.

6 Release pressure and let cool for 20 minutes. Unlock lid.

7 Slice roast and serve warm topped with cooked mushrooms and radishes.

Pantry Staples

olive oil, vegetable broth

NET CARBS

1G

SERVES 8

PER SERVING	
CALORIES	254
FAT	12G
PROTEIN	32G
SODIUM	941MG
FIBER	1G
CARBOHYDRATES	2G
NET CARBS	1G
SUGAR	1G
SUGAR ALCOHOL	0G

TIME

PREP TIME:	10 MINUTES
COOK TIME:	29 MINUTES

TIPS & OPTIONS

How "done" do you like your tri-tip? Check the internal temperature; you'll want it at 135°F for medium rare or 150°F for medium. Beyond that, it's on you.

Let cooked meat "sit" in its juices for a while prior to cutting.

You can easily modify the cook method here. Simply wrap the roast in tin foil and bake in the oven low and slow, a 250°F oven temperature until internal temperature of meat reaches 135°F for medium rare or 150°F for medium.

For melt-in-your-mouth tenderness, cut the tri-tip across the grain.

salt, ground black pepper, olive oil

NET CARBS

1G

SERVES 4

PER SERVING	
CALORIES	505
FAT	32G
PROTEIN	42G
SODIUM	1,276MG
FIBER	0G
CARBOHYDRATES	1G
NET CARBS	1G
SUGAR	0G
SUGAR ALCOHOL	0G

TIME

PREP TIME:	10 MINUTES
COOK TIME:	60 MINUTES

TIPS & OPTIONS

I often use spice blends to save time and space in my kitchen. Poultry seasoning is one I use often to flavor chicken, turkey, or even pork. Depending on the brand, I expect it to contain thyme, sage, marjoram, coriander, and/or rosemary.

If your grill flares up, pour a little beer on top. My dad taught me this trick; it's very effective!

If bad weather spoils your outdoor cooking plans, you can always bake the chicken at 350°F until internal temperature of meat reaches 165°F.

DANCING DRUNKEN CHICKEN

Barbecuing is more fun when you hold a spatula in one hand and an ice-cold beer in the other. Just because you're losing weight doesn't mean you can't enjoy a "chilly one"! There are plenty of low-carb beers on the market to choose from. Corona Premier, Michelob Ultra, and Miller Lite are just a few of my favorites, all 3g net carbs per 12-ounce can. Pull a can off of your six-pack and set it aside to make Dancing Drunken Chicken. You won't be disappointed!

- **2 teaspoons salt**
- **½ teaspoon ground black pepper**
- **1½ teaspoons poultry seasoning**
- **1 (3½-pound) whole chicken**
- **2 tablespoons olive oil**
- **1 (12-ounce) can low-carb beer**

1   Preheat outdoor grill over medium heat. Line a small baking sheet with foil.

2   In a small bowl, combine salt, black pepper, and poultry seasoning.

3   Brush exterior of chicken with oil and rub seasonings over exterior as well as interior of chicken.

4   Open beer and take a nice-sized swig, at least 1 ounce. Stand beer on the prepared baking sheet and slide the whole chicken completely over the can.

5   Move the baking sheet to the grill and cook chicken with the lid down 45–60 minutes until internal temperature is at least 165°F.

6   Remove from the grill. When cool enough to handle, cut and serve.

CON COCONUT SHRIMP

When I discovered my grocery store sold fresh skewered shrimp, five for a dollar, I was hooked—fish, line, and sinker (oh, such a bad joke!). Seriously, though. Seafood that's affordable and conveniently packaged is a goldmine. My family doesn't always agree with the smell of cooking fish, though, so I've learned to cook it virtually odor-free in my air fryer. There is never a complaint when I make Con Coconut Shrimp!

- ✦ 1 cup superfine blanched almond flour
- ✦ ¼ teaspoon salt
- ✦ ⅛ teaspoon ground black pepper
- 3 large eggs, beaten
- 1 tablespoon heavy whipping cream
- 1 cup shredded unsweetened coconut
- ✦ 3 tablespoons 0g net carbs sweetener
- 24 jumbo (21–25 per pound) peeled, deveined, and cooked shrimp

1 Set out two dinner plates and one medium bowl. On one plate, combine flour, salt, and pepper. In the medium bowl, whisk eggs and cream. On the second plate, mix coconut with sweetener.

2 First, coat both sides of each shrimp in the flour mixture. Next, dip shrimp in the egg wash and shake off excess. Finally, press both sides of each shrimp into the sweetened coconut mixture.

3 Spread out 6–8 shrimp on the crisper tray of an air fryer and cook 10 minutes at 400°F. Remove and transfer shrimp to a clean plate. Repeat until all shrimp are cooked.

4 Divide evenly among four plates and serve warm.

Pantry Staples

superfine blanched almond flour, salt, ground black pepper, 0g net carbs sweetener

NET CARBS

2G

SERVES 4

PER SERVING	
CALORIES	229
FAT	13G
PROTEIN	20G
SODIUM	741MG
FIBER	3G
CARBOHYDRATES	10G
NET CARBS	2G
SUGAR	1G
SUGAR ALCOHOL	5G

TIME

PREP TIME:	10 MINUTES
COOK TIME:	40 MINUTES

TIPS & OPTIONS

Depending on the size of your air fryer and what accessories you have, it's possible to cook a larger quantity of food at once. Keep in mind that food inside an air fryer needs to be well spaced out to cook effectively.

If you like the mix of sweet and salty, try dipping your shrimp in Pickle-Tickled Ranch Dressing (see Chapter 5).

If you don't have an air fryer, oven bake shrimp at 400°F until internal temperature of shrimp reaches 145°F.

0g net carbs sweetener

NET CARBS

1G

SERVES 4

PER SERVING

CALORIES	215
FAT	14G
PROTEIN	18G
SODIUM	231MG
FIBER	1G
CARBOHYDRATES	2G
NET CARBS	1G
SUGAR	1G
SUGAR ALCOHOL	0G

TIME

PREP TIME:	15 MINUTES
COOK TIME:	0 MINUTES

TIPS & OPTIONS

If you prefer to double-dip, double up on the cranberry and mayonnaise mixture and place the remaining portion in a small bowl (in the center of your platter). Don't forget a spoon! We are civilized, after all.

Not a fan of feta? Substitute Gorgonzola cheese instead.

For added crunch, sprinkle chopped walnuts or pecans on top of your lettuce cups. Delicious, right?

TALKIN' TURKEY WRAPS

The mystery of what to do with Thanksgiving turkey leftovers has been solved. Somebody alert Raymond Burr! What I love about these turkey "sandwiches" is how easily they are gobbled up. (I know, I know…that was a bad one.) I can set out a tray of Talkin' Turkey Wraps for my family to eat, and they're gone before dinner is even served. Do I complain? Nope! I just *happen* to have more turkey available. (Why did I buy a 25-pound turkey?) I can easily assemble another platter.

8 large butter lettuce leaves

½ pound roasted turkey, chopped into small pieces no larger than ½"

⅓ cup fresh cranberries

¼ cup full-fat mayonnaise

✦ 2 (1-gram) packets 0g net carbs sweetener

¼ cup full-fat feta cheese, crumbled

1 On a large platter, artfully arrange butter lettuce leaves.

2 Evenly divide the turkey among the lettuce cups.

3 In a small bowl, mash cranberries with a fork. Add mayonnaise and sweetener and stir until blended.

4 Dollop each turkey cup with even amounts of cranberry mixture (about 2 teaspoons each).

5 Sprinkle even amounts of feta cheese on top of each lettuce cup. Serve immediately.

NET CARBS

5G

SERVES 4

PER SERVING	
CALORIES	290
FAT	21G
PROTEIN	18G
SODIUM	953MG
FIBER	1G
CARBOHYDRATES	6G
NET CARBS	5G
SUGAR	3G
SUGAR ALCOHOL	0G

TIME

PREP TIME:	10 MINUTES
COOK TIME:	13 MINUTES

TIPS & OPTIONS

Top with a sprinkle of freshly diced Roma tomatoes. These have a tougher skin and therefore hold their shape better when diced into small pieces. Use a serrated knife for an easier slice and dice.

SKEDADDLIN' SHRIMP SCAMPI

I remember the day I bought a commercial zoodle maker. I was so excited to fork over a crisp twenty-dollar bill with a Bed Bath & Beyond coupon and skedaddle home to make pasta. PASTA! I hadn't eaten spaghetti in (what seemed like) decades. Boy, was I in for a big treat…or should I say a giant mess? The contraption was difficult to use (and even harder to clean). My mom had a good chuckle and introduced me to the timeless julienne peeler. Good kitchen tools never go out of style, just like this shrimp scampi dish!

- **3 tablespoons olive oil**
- **1 pound medium (41–60 per pound) shrimp, peeled and deveined**
- **2 teaspoons 100% lemon juice**
- **¼ teaspoon garlic powder**
- **¼ teaspoon salt**
- **⅛ teaspoon ground black pepper**
- **2 medium zucchini, peeled into zoodles with a julienne peeler**
- **3 tablespoons Pesto from Cool As a Cucumber Pesto Salad (see Chapter 5)**
- **2 tablespoons grated Parmesan cheese**

1 In a large skillet over medium heat, heat oil. Add shrimp, lemon juice, garlic powder, salt, and pepper and cook 5–7 minutes until shrimp is cooked through, stirring regularly.

2 Microwave zoodles in a large microwave-safe bowl 4 minutes until tender. Drain excess water and add zoodles to shrimp mixture on stovetop.

3 Add Pesto and gently stir until evenly coated, 1–2 minutes.

4 Divide scampi evenly on four dinner plates and top with equal amounts Parmesan cheese. Serve warm.

CHAPTER 10

DESSERTS AND DRINKS

At the beginning of my weight loss journey, I removed all tempting sweets from my house. Sure, that probably wasn't fair to the rest of my family (apparently, access to Chips Ahoy! was an unspoken wedding vow?). *Whatever.* I learned very quickly (as in within the first hour) that eliminating *100 percent* of all tempting food and drinks around me increased my chances of dieting success by, well, 100 percent. If I didn't buy a 2-liter of Pepsi, then I couldn't drink it. Problem solved. *Yeah, right!* Let's be realistic. I could only control my home environment to a limited extent. Plus, I had to leave the house at some point. Then what?

Distraction has been the least effective strategy for me. I've tried chewing sugar-free gum, learning a musical instrument, even brushing my teeth after dinner—anything to keep my mind off sugar. My success rate with the distraction method, I'll admit, is pretty low. You see, for decades, I enjoyed eating something sweet after dinner. No matter how many times I started a craft to distract my fingers, I kept finding myself back in the kitchen.

I wish I was one of those people who could moderate their intake of sweets. Some people can have "just a bite" and feel satisfied. Not me! As a child, I remember eating just a bite of the forbidden cake in the fridge…and then another, and another, and another…trying to make a clean line of bites *all in a row* to hide my tracks. One bite, even of "the good stuff," has never been enough for me. One bite always started an avalanche; I couldn't stop myself.

Eventually, I learned I had to stop beating myself up about enjoying sweets if I was ever going to be successful with weight loss.

My personality is not one to cut, moderate, or distract itself from enjoying taboo foods. *No ma'am!*

I needed to find a way to indulge guilty pleasures that wouldn't sabotage my efforts at weight loss. With DIRTY, LAZY, KETO, I found a workable solution!

No matter what confections I'm craving, I've learned how to make a quick-fix, low-carb substitute. In addition to curbing my sweet tooth, I no longer feel deprived or ashamed. That, my friends, is the ultimate taste of sweet success.

DISCOMBOBULATED DONUT HOLES

With DIRTY, LAZY, KETO, you don't have to feel like you're missing out. There is always a way to make your favorite carbolicious treats in a modified, low-carb way. Take these cinnamon-sugar donut holes, for example. I've cut out the sugar and wheat flour here but maintained all the traditional donut flavor and moist texture. "Do-nut" look so discombobulated! Believe me when I tell you it's possible to make a heavenly, low-carb donut. Pour yourself a cup of coffee, sit back, and enjoy this surprising treat.

- 1 cup superfine blanched almond flour
- 4 tablespoons 0g net carbs sweetener, divided
- 3 tablespoons unsalted butter, melted and divided
- 1 teaspoon ground cinnamon, divided
- 1 tablespoon flax meal (ground flaxseed)
- 2 tablespoons water
- ⅛ teaspoon salt

1 Preheat oven to 350°F. Line a baking sheet with parchment paper.

2 In a large mixing bowl, combine flour, 3 tablespoons sweetener, 2 tablespoons butter, ¾ teaspoon cinnamon, flax meal, water, and salt. Mix until dough forms.

3 Evenly scoop into eight round balls and place balls on the prepared baking sheet, spaced out so they don't touch.

4 Bake 10–12 minutes, turning halfway through.

5 Remove from oven and let cool.

6 Add remaining 1 tablespoon butter to a small bowl.

7 In a separate small bowl, combine remaining 1 tablespoon sweetener and ¼ teaspoon cinnamon.

8 Dip cooled donut holes into the butter and gently shake to remove excess. Transfer donuts to the cinnamon-sugar mixture. Use a spoon to fully coat the outside of each donut.

9 Transfer coated donuts to a serving plate and serve warm.

Pantry Staples

superfine blanched almond flour, 0g net carbs sweetener, salt

NET CARBS

2G

SERVES 4

PER SERVING

CALORIES	272
FAT	24G
PROTEIN	6G
SODIUM	73MG
FIBER	4G
CARBOHYDRATES	12G
NET CARBS	2G
SUGAR	1G
SUGAR ALCOHOL	6G

TIME

PREP TIME:	10 MINUTES
COOK TIME:	12 MINUTES

TIPS & OPTIONS

If you haven't picked up a bag of flax meal yet, do so now. Today is your opportunity to road test this amazing ingredient! Chock-full of protein and healthy fats, flax meal serves as a binder in foods that might otherwise fall apart.

Serve your donut holes with a cup of Bulletproof coffee; this breakfast will leave you satisfied and full for hours.

PERSONAL PUMPKIN PIE

This year, I learned how to make pumpkin purée from scratch. I don't know WHAT got into me? Maybe it was because I brought the fresh pumpkin home from an actual pumpkin patch....I don't know. Before I had time to think, I was cutting, cleaning, and roasting pumpkin meat. Do you know what it tasted like? *Exactly the same as the stuff from the can.* Cut some corners, my friend. Leave your pumpkin outside the front door and open a can of puréed pumpkin to make this no-frills pumpkin pie!

Crust
- 1½ cups superfine blanched almond flour
- ½ cup unsalted butter, softened
- ½ cup 0g net carbs sweetener
- ¼ teaspoon salt

Filling
- ¾ cup canned 100% pure pumpkin purée
- ¼ cup heavy whipping cream
- 3 tablespoons 0g net carbs sweetener
- 1 large egg
- 1 teaspoon pumpkin pie spice
- ¼ teaspoon salt
- ¼ teaspoon pure vanilla extract

1. Preheat oven to 425°F. Lightly spray a twelve-hole muffin pan with nonstick cooking spray.

2. In a medium bowl, combine all ingredients for the Crust. Press equal amounts of Crust mixture into twelve muffin cups. Use your thumbs to create a bird's-nest shape.

3. Bake 9–10 minutes until edges start browning.

4. Remove from oven and decrease oven temperature to 350°F.

5. Next, make the Filling. In a medium mixing bowl, use a mixer to blend all Filling ingredients.

6. Use an ice cream scoop to transfer equal amounts of Filling into the prepared Crusts.

7. Bake 27–30 minutes. Check doneness by pushing a toothpick into the center of a "pie." It's done if the toothpick comes out dry.

8. Remove from the oven and let cool. Serve warm.

Pantry Staples

superfine blanched almond flour, 0g net carbs sweetener, salt, pure vanilla extract

NET CARBS
3G

SERVES 12

PER SERVING

CALORIES	193
FAT	17G
PROTEIN	4G
SODIUM	106MG
FIBER	2G
CARBOHYDRATES	10G
NET CARBS	3G
SUGAR	1G
SUGAR ALCOHOL	5G

TIME

PREP TIME:	15 MINUTES
COOK TIME:	40 MINUTES

TIPS & OPTIONS

Top each mini pie with a pecan half.

Buy spice blends (like pumpkin pie spice) to save time and space. It's four spices in one: cinnamon, ginger, nutmeg, and allspice.

Top your pie with— you guessed it— (unsweetened) canned dairy whipped topping!

Making miniature pies in muffin pans helps me maintain a sense of portion control. Besides, individual "pies" are extra cute.

CHILLY CHEESECAKE BARS

Pantry Staples

superfine blanched almond flour, 0g net carbs sweetener, pure vanilla extract, sugar-free chocolate chips

NET CARBS

6G

SERVES 8

PER SERVING	
CALORIES	413
FAT	35G
PROTEIN	8G
SODIUM	191MG
FIBER	5G
CARBOHYDRATES	17G
NET CARBS	6G
SUGAR	2G
SUGAR ALCOHOL	6G

TIME

PREP TIME:	10 MINUTES
COOK TIME:	50 MINUTES, PLUS 30 MINUTES CHILLING TIME

TIPS & OPTIONS »

Instead of chocolate chips, try substituting an equal amount of fresh blueberries. Be sure to carefully fold them into the batter, or else you risk serving a completely blue dessert. Unless you're serving Smurfs, blue food is just not appetizing!

It's tempting for me to overeat DIRTY, LAZY, KETO desserts. I will always love my sweets! I have to remind myself that sugar-free doesn't mean a free-for-all. I admit that sometimes I have a REALLY HARD TIME stopping after just one serving! If you're like me, and low-carb baked goods are a trigger, try limiting your exposure altogether. Put your cravings on ice by saving desserts like Chilly Cheesecake Bars for special (aka desperate) occasions.

- **1 cup superfine blanched almond flour**
- **7 tablespoons unsalted butter, melted**
- **8 tablespoons 0g net carbs sweetener, divided**
- **14 ounces full-fat cream cheese, softened**
- **1 large egg, beaten**
- **2 teaspoons pure vanilla extract**
- **1 teaspoon 100% lemon juice**
- **½ cup sugar-free chocolate chips**

1 Preheat oven to 370°F. Grease a 9" × 5" loaf pan.

2 In a medium bowl, combine flour, butter, and 2 tablespoons sweetener. Transfer to loaf pan and press evenly into bottom.

3 Bake 5 minutes. Remove from oven.

4 In a medium mixing bowl, add remaining ingredients except chocolate chips. Use a mixer to combine, stopping to scrape the sides of the bowl and the beaters. Fold in chocolate chips.

5 Transfer the mixture to the loaf pan, pouring over the crust, and bake covered 40–45 minutes until firm.

6 Remove from the oven and transfer to the refrigerator. Let chill 30 minutes. Cut into eight bars. Serve cold.

NET CARBS

9G

SERVES 2

PER SERVING	
CALORIES	171
FAT	8G
PROTEIN	11G
SODIUM	41MG
FIBER	3G
CARBOHYDRATES	14G
NET CARBS	9G
SUGAR	7G
SUGAR ALCOHOL	2G

TIME

PREP TIME:	5 MINUTES, PLUS 30 MINUTES FREEZING TIME
COOK TIME:	0 MINUTES

TIPS & OPTIONS

Sprinkle your sundae with a smidge of pretzel dust (ya know, from the bottom of the bag?) for a salty-sweet effect.

Ta da! Drizzle with Runner-Up Strawberry Syrup (see Chapter 4) for added flair.

Serve in a parfait cup and enjoy with an extra-long spoon? *Now you're talkin'!*

STRAWBERRY FREEZY

One of the many benefits of DIRTY, LAZY, KETO is its flexibility. You can "spend your carbs" as you see fit *without any judgment*! I find that point to be empowering. If I want to enjoy a strawberry frozen yogurt sundae dessert for breakfast (which admittedly I have done many times), no one will stop me. Go ahead and live on the edge, enjoy this Strawberry Freezy any time of day.

> 1 cup sliced frozen strawberries
>
> 5 (1-gram) packets 0g net carbs sweetener
>
> 1 cup full-fat, plain, Greek-style yogurt
>
> 2 teaspoons pure vanilla extract
>
> 1 tablespoon sugar-free chocolate chips

1 Add all ingredients except chocolate chips to a blender. Pulse blender 30 seconds until mixture is creamy.

2 Divide into two dessert bowls and put in the freezer for 30 minutes.

3 Top each serving with equal amounts of chocolate chips. Serve immediately.

KINDA CANNOLI

A traditional Italian cannoli is made with a crispy fried shell stuffed with rich mascarpone or ricotta cheese. My quickie version may not be as *autentico,* but it sings all the same high notes (and is ready to eat a lot faster). It's likely you already have everything you need on hand to quickly make this decadent DLK version of a classic cannoli.

Chaffles

- 2 tablespoons unsalted butter, softened
- 2 large eggs, beaten
- 1 tablespoon 0g net carbs sweetener
- 3 tablespoons superfine blanched almond flour
- ¼ teaspoon baking powder
- ½ teaspoon pure vanilla extract

Cannoli Topping

- 1½ tablespoons sugar-free chocolate chips, divided
- 1½ tablespoons 4% milkfat cottage cheese
- 1 tablespoon full-fat cream cheese, softened
- 1½ tablespoons 0g net carbs sweetener
- ½ teaspoon pure vanilla extract

1 Spray a waffle maker with nonstick cooking spray and preheat.

2 Make the Chaffles. In a medium bowl, combine all Chaffle ingredients and whisk until creamy.

3 Evenly distribute batter into two waffle molds and cook 3–4 minutes. Remove Chaffles and transfer to two serving plates.

4 Next, make the Cannoli Topping. In a small microwave-safe bowl, heat 1 tablespoon chocolate chips 30–60 seconds, stopping to stir halfway through. Stir until creamy and chocolate is fully melted.

5 In a second small bowl, combine all remaining Cannoli Topping ingredients except remaining chocolate chips and stir. Add melted chocolate and stir until mixture is creamy.

6 Create a sling with each Chaffle by folding the opposite corners together. Stuff each Chaffle with equal amounts of Cannoli Topping and pin the Chaffle ends together with toothpicks. Sprinkle remaining chocolate chips onto the exposed Cannoli Topping.

7 Transfer to the refrigerator to chill at least 30 minutes. Serve cold.

Pantry Staples

0g net carbs sweetener, superfine blanched almond flour, baking powder, pure vanilla extract, sugar-free chocolate chips

NET CARBS

2G

SERVES 2

PER SERVING

CALORIES	329
FAT	26G
PROTEIN	11G
SODIUM	197MG
FIBER	4G
CARBOHYDRATES	16G
NET CARBS	2G
SUGAR	1G
SUGAR ALCOHOL	10G

TIME

PREP TIME: 10 MINUTES
COOK TIME: 5 MINUTES,
PLUS 30 MINUTES CHILLING TIME

≪ TIPS & OPTIONS

Use a plastic fork to remove the Chaffles from the waffle maker to prevent scratching the Teflon surface.

Take a shortcut and stuff your Kinda Cannoli with leftover Homey Honey-Walnut Cream Cheese (see Chapter 4).

Dust the cannoli and the surrounding plate with a hint of 100% cocoa powder. Place a single mint leaf on the cannoli.

STUFFED BIRTHDAY CAKE SURPRISE

How will you celebrate your DIRTY, LAZY, KETO birthday differently this year? Instead of going off the rails, I'd like to suggest enjoying a sugar-free cupcake or a fun activity instead. Over the years, I've come up with some real birthday wingdings including: hiking to the top of a 1,000-foot waterfall in Yosemite and biking across the Golden Gate Bridge in San Francisco!

Pantry Staples

0g net carbs sweetener, pure vanilla extract, baking powder, salt, superfine blanched almond flour

NET CARBS

3G

SERVES 10

PER SERVING	
CALORIES	238
FAT	19G
PROTEIN	5G
SODIUM	210MG
FIBER	2G
CARBOHYDRATES	19G
NET CARBS	3G
SUGAR	2G
SUGAR ALCOHOL	14G

TIME

PREP TIME:	25 MINUTES
COOK TIME:	20 MINUTES

TIPS & OPTIONS

If strawberry isn't your favorite flavor, you can substitute something else as your cupcake surprise. Sugar-free chocolate chips or a dollop of no-sugar-added nut butter? Be sure to insert it while the cupcake is still warm so the surprise quickly melts when "plugged" with cake.

For me, the size of a cupcake offers a little bit of built-in portion control. I have to stop and say "Hmmmm…" before unwrapping another, which often is enough of a pause to help knock some common sense into me.

Cupcakes

¼ cup unsalted butter, softened

4 ounces full-fat cream cheese, softened

½ cup 0g net carbs sweetener

½ teaspoon pure vanilla extract

2 large eggs

½ tablespoon baking powder

¼ teaspoon salt

1¼ cups superfine blanched almond flour

Pink Frosting

1 cup 0g net carbs sweetener

2 ounces full-fat cream cheese, softened

3 tablespoons heavy whipping cream

1 teaspoon pure vanilla extract

1 tablespoon Runner-Up Strawberry Syrup (see Chapter 4)

Strawberry Filling

5 tablespoons Runner-Up Strawberry Syrup (see Chapter 4)

1 Preheat oven to 375°F. Line a muffin pan with ten muffin liners.

2 Make the Cupcakes. In a medium mixing bowl, combine butter, cream cheese, sweetener, vanilla, and eggs. Beat with a mixer until batter is smooth.

3 Add baking powder and salt. Mix again, scraping the sides of the bowl often.

4 Add almond flour and continue to mix until thoroughly combined. Evenly distribute Cupcake batter into ten liners.

5 Bake 15–20 minutes until a toothpick inserted in the middle comes out dry. Remove from the oven and let cool. Remove Cupcakes from the pan.

(continued)

6   Next, make the Pink Frosting. In a small bowl, combine all Frosting ingredients except Runner-Up Strawberry Syrup and whisk until thoroughly combined. Add Runner-Up Strawberry Syrup gradually until you reach an attractive shade of pink.

7   Use a vegetable peeler to remove a column of cake from the top center of each Cupcake measuring ¾" wide × 1" deep (save the carved-out pieces). Fill each Cupcake hole with even amounts of Strawberry Filling, about 1 teaspoon per cupcake, then plug the holes with the removed cake.

8   Scoop Pink Frosting into a piping bag (or Ziploc bag with a corner cut) and evenly spread onto tops of Cupcakes, leaving the liners on.

9   Serve immediately or store in an airtight container in the refrigerator.

BEST ATTEMPT RICE PUDDING

Over the years, I've tried to replicate my mother's rice pudding. The results, I'm sorry to say, have often missed the mark! Like tapioca, traditional rice pudding has a unique consistency that's hard to replicate. I kept thinking it was my measuring that was off, but in reality, it was something much deeper. I finally realized that no dessert recipe would be able to capture the nostalgic memories of cooking with my mom. Best Attempt Rice Pudding is not an exact replica of my childhood favorite, but considering the drastic reduction in carbs this recipe provides me, I'll take it!

¼ cup frozen riced cauliflower

1 teaspoon whole white chia seeds

1 tablespoon unsweetened vanilla almond milk

1 teaspoon heavy whipping cream

2 (1-gram) packets 0g net carbs sweetener

⅛ teaspoon ground cinnamon

1 In a small microwave-safe glass bowl, microwave cauliflower 30 seconds.

2 Add all remaining ingredients and stir. Set aside 5 minutes until chia softens.

3 Serve immediately.

Pantry Staples

0g net carbs sweetener

NET CARBS

2G

SERVES 1

PER SERVING	
CALORIES	72
FAT	5G
PROTEIN	2G
SODIUM	18MG
FIBER	4G
CARBOHYDRATES	6G
NET CARBS	2G
SUGAR	1G
SUGAR ALCOHOL	0G

TIME

PREP TIME:	2 MINUTES, PLUS 5 MINUTES RESTING TIME
COOK TIME:	30 SECONDS

TIPS & OPTIONS

Serve warm or cold, depending on your preference.

You can use black or white chia seeds for this dish. I happen to think the white chia seeds look more appealing here.

n/a

NET CARBS

0G

SERVES 4

PER SERVING

CALORIES	17
FAT	0G
PROTEIN	4G
SODIUM	39MG
FIBER	0G
CARBOHYDRATES	0G
NET CARBS	0G
SUGAR	0G
SUGAR ALCOHOL	0G

TIME

PREP TIME:	15 MINUTES, PLUS 2 HOURS CHILLING TIME
COOK TIME:	0 MINUTES

TIPS & OPTIONS »

Wash the eyedropper immediately after use to prevent gelatin from drying inside.

Young children love to help make this dessert. Keep multiple eyedroppers on hand for little helpers to use.

Make a variety of gummy bear flavors and colors using your favorite sugar-free gelatin flavors (or, in my case, whatever flavor is on sale). Sugar-free gelatin is sold in a variety of flavors: cherry, lemon, lime, orange, raspberry, strawberry, and more!

SKINNY GUMMY BEARS

Gummy bears are a beloved candy many of us don't want to let go of. In my *Facebook* support group for DIRTY, LAZY, KETO, I frequently hear tales-gone-wrong of members overindulging on these sugar-free candies ordered from the Internet. These must contain an *offending* ingredient, as unexpected, explosive intestinal consequences are often reported. That's not fun! My innocent Skinny Gummy Bears are just as tasty and colorful as the original candy we all adore but won't leave you experiencing a tummy ache.

> **1 cup water**
>
> **2 teaspoons sugar-free plain gelatin, divided**
>
> **2 teaspoons sugar-free flavored gelatin, divided (½ teaspoon cherry, ½ teaspoon lime, ½ teaspoon orange, ½ teaspoon lemon)**

1. In a small saucepan, boil water.

2. Set out four small glass bowls and add ½ teaspoon plain gelatin to each. Then add ½ teaspoon of different-flavored gelatin powders to each bowl.

3. Add ¼ cup of the boiling water to each bowl. Slowly stir until gelatin is completely dissolved, 30–60 seconds.

4. Spray four silicone gummy bear candy molds (50 gummy bear shapes per mold) with nonstick cooking spray.

5. Using an eyedropper, fill the gummy bear molds with the gelatin mixtures. Do not overfill. Refrigerate 2 hours until fully hardened.

6. Pop the gummy bears out of the molds. Mix the colors evenly into four servings and enjoy immediately.

DOUBLE CHOCOLATE AHOY COOKIES

I used to eat Chips Ahoy! by the sleeve (not cookie). My husband loved them just as much. To his dismay, when I began my weight loss journey, I had to get rid of those tempting cookies altogether. I tried relocating them to a hard-to-reach location, like the cabinet above the fridge, but that didn't work. I would just stand on a chair to reach them! I don't want to feel that out of control around sweets ever again. Now, even when I make sugar-free Double Chocolate Ahoy Cookies, I immediately package them in single-serving bags and store extras in the bottom of the freezer.

- **6 tablespoons unsalted butter, melted**
- **1 large egg**
- **1 teaspoon pure vanilla extract**
- **9 tablespoons 0g net carbs sweetener, divided**
- **2 cups superfine blanched almond flour**
- **1 teaspoon baking powder**
- **⅛ teaspoon salt**
- **½ cup sugar-free chocolate chips**
- **½ tablespoon 100% cocoa powder**

1   Preheat oven to 370°F. Line a baking sheet with parchment paper.

2   In a large mixing bowl, combine butter, egg, vanilla, and ½ cup (8 tablespoons) sweetener and beat with a mixer 1–2 minutes until smooth.

3   Slowly beat in flour, baking powder, and salt until well blended and a batter forms. Fold in chocolate chips.

4   In a small bowl, combine cocoa powder and remaining 1 tablespoon sweetener. Scoop out 1" balls of dough and roll them in the cocoa mixture until completely covered.

5   Place balls spread out on the prepared baking sheet. Using your thumb, press down slightly on each ball to create a traditional cookie shape (cookies will not rise much).

6   Bake 15–17 minutes until cookies are firm and starting to brown. Serve warm.

Pantry Staples

pure vanilla extract, 0g net carbs sweetener, superfine blanched almond flour, baking powder, salt, sugar-free chocolate chips

NET CARBS

1G

SERVES 24

PER SERVING	
CALORIES	109
FAT	9G
PROTEIN	3G
SODIUM	35MG
FIBER	2G
CARBOHYDRATES	6G
NET CARBS	1G
SUGAR	0G
SUGAR ALCOHOL	3G

TIME

PREP TIME:	15 MINUTES
COOK TIME:	17 MINUTES

TIPS & OPTIONS

Cookies are best enjoyed with a cold glass of milk. One of my favorites is Silk brand unsweetened vanilla almond milk (1g net carbs per 1-cup serving), or you can make your own Mo Milk (see recipe in this chapter).

Traditionalists may omit rolling the cookie in the cocoa and sweetener mix.

An alternative to chocolate chips is to add walnut or pecan pieces. Since you're going the "healthy" route, add a tablespoon or two of flaxseeds. Now you've created a power cookie!

Pantry Staples

n/a

NET CARBS

3G

SERVES 8

PER SERVING

CALORIES	82
FAT	6G
PROTEIN	2G
SODIUM	77MG
FIBER	0G
CARBOHYDRATES	3G
NET CARBS	3G
SUGAR	2G
SUGAR ALCOHOL	0G

TIME

PREP TIME:	20 MINUTES, PLUS 4 HOURS CHILLING TIME
COOK TIME:	0 MINUTES

TIPS & OPTIONS »

Depending on the crowd (or how tipsy I expect they might get at dinner), I will serve this dish in disposable, clear plastic cups from the dollar store. This makes for less breakage of my glasses (and, subsequently, a much easier cleanup).

Enjoy this dish year-round by substituting the strawberry and lime flavors with another colorful combination of the numerous available flavors of sugar-free gelatin.

CHRISTMAS DESSERT SALAD

Midwesterners like me consider Jell-O a salad, not a dessert (or maybe that's only at my house?). Either way, the more Jell-O at the table, the better. My Aunt Ted took her gelatin "salad" to the next level, adding sour cream AND whipped cream. *That's what I'm talkin' 'bout!* Made with strawberry- and lime-flavored gelatin, Christmas Dessert Salad looks festive and tastes great.

> **2 cups boiling water, divided**
> **1 (0.3-ounce) box sugar-free strawberry gelatin mix**
> **2 cups cold water, divided**
> **1 (0.3-ounce) box sugar-free lime gelatin mix**
> **1 cup full-fat sour cream**
> **1 cup unsweetened canned dairy whipped topping**
> **2 tablespoons crushed pretzels**

1 In a medium heat-safe bowl, carefully stir together 1 cup boiling water and strawberry gelatin until gelatin is dissolved.

2 Add 1 cup cold water and stir to combine.

3 Pour ¼ cup strawberry gelatin mix into each of eight parfait cups. Clean the bowl. Cover the cups with plastic wrap and refrigerate 4 hours until firm.

4 In the same bowl, stir to combine remaining 1 cup boiling water and lime gelatin mix. Stir until gelatin is dissolved. Stir in remaining 1 cup cold water. Cover with plastic wrap and refrigerate 4 hours until firm.

5 Top each cup of set strawberry gelatin with 2 tablespoons sour cream.

6 Stir set lime gelatin while still in the medium bowl until it's a uniform consistency of approximately ½" chunks. Add ¼ cup lime gelatin to each parfait cup.

7 Top each parfait cup with 2 tablespoons whipped topping. Finally, sprinkle even amounts of crushed pretzels on top of each cup. Serve immediately while still chilled.

DLK PSL (PUMPKIN SPICE LATTE)

Finding the necessary ingredients to make a gourmet coffee used to be stressful for me—my spice rack is a disaster! To solve this problem, I splurged on a second set of favorite coffee additives (which I hide next to the coffee pot). Who cares if you have duplicate bottles of cinnamon, pumpkin pie spice, vanilla, and cocoa powder? Organize your kitchen to make cooking more convenient, I say! Now that I can find what I'm looking for, I've become a more efficient (and happier) barista. Taste the proof with this amazing low-carb DLK PSL (Pumpkin Spice Latte) recipe, better than any drive-thru.

- **2 cups unsweetened coffee**
- **½ cup heavy whipping cream**
- **½ cup canned 100% pure pumpkin purée**
- **1 teaspoon pumpkin pie spice**
- **2 teaspoons pure vanilla extract**
- **2 tablespoons unsalted butter, melted**
- **3 tablespoons 0g net carbs sweetener**

1 To a blender, add all ingredients and pulse until thoroughly mixed.

2 Evenly pour mixture into two oversized microwave-safe coffee mugs.

3 Microwave each 45 seconds. Serve warm.

Pantry Staples

pure vanilla extract, 0g net carbs sweetener

NET CARBS

6G

SERVES 2

PER SERVING	
CALORIES	357
FAT	32G
PROTEIN	2G
SODIUM	31MG
FIBER	2G
CARBOHYDRATES	17G
NET CARBS	6G
SUGAR	5G
SUGAR ALCOHOL	9G

TIME

PREP TIME:	10 MINUTES
COOK TIME:	0 MINUTES

TIPS & OPTIONS

Optional toppings are sprinkled ground cinnamon, a dollop of canned dairy whipped topping (unsweetened), or for those feeling wild and crazy today, a quick dusting of 100% cocoa powder.

If you prefer your DLK PSL to have a bold, unsweetened flavor, reduce the amount of 0g net carbs sweetener in this recipe to only 1 tablespoon.

MOMMY'S SPECIAL POPSICLES

NET CARBS

3G

SERVES 6

PER SERVING

CALORIES	79
FAT	1G
PROTEIN	2G
SODIUM	63MG
FIBER	3G
CARBOHYDRATES	6G
NET CARBS	3G
SUGAR	2G
SUGAR ALCOHOL	0G

TIME

PREP TIME: 10 MINUTES, PLUS 45 MINUTES CHILLING TIME AND 3 HOURS FREEZING TIME

COOK TIME: 0 MINUTES

TIPS & OPTIONS »

Any low-carb fruit can be used in this Popsicle recipe. Blackberries, with 6g net carbs per 1-cup serving, would make a nice choice.

If you don't have a traditional Popsicle mold on hand (who does?), think outside the box. I use a mini silicone muffin pan, which I purchased for my Instant Pot®.

If a Popsicle gets stuck in the mold, try running the outside of the mold under hot water until it loosens and/or twist the mold like an ice cube tray.

My husband calls all berries "nature's candy." He thinks lower-carb fruits like strawberries and blueberries are ridiculously sweet. Is he crazy or what? Apparently, he didn't spend his youth like I did. My favorite childhood candy included sucking on a finger dipped in Kool-Aid mix. Maybe my taste buds are fried from decades of misuse, but I prefer my desserts *extra sweet*. The combination of fruit with sweetener here makes Mommy's Special Popsicles taste just like candy. Plus, there is an added secret ingredient reserved just for grownups!

½ cup boiling water

1 (0.3-ounce) box sugar-free raspberry gelatin mix

1 pint ripe raspberries

20 drops liquid 0g net carbs sweetener

1 tablespoon heavy whipping cream

3 fluid ounces (2 shots) plain vodka

1 In a medium heat-safe glass bowl, combine water and gelatin mix. Stir until gelatin is completely dissolved. Cover and refrigerate until semi-gelatinous, 45 minutes.

2 To a blender, add berries, sweetener, cream, and vodka and pulse 30–60 seconds until creamy and smooth.

3 Whisk berry mixture into gelatin mixture.

4 Spray six mini Popsicle molds with nonstick cooking spray. Evenly pour the mixture into the Popsicle molds and freeze 2–3 hours until firm. When firm enough, after 30–45 minutes, push a Popsicle stick approximately 1½" into each Popsicle.

5 Remove Popsicles from the freezer 20–30 minutes prior to desired eating time (this allows Popsicles to slightly thaw, making removal from the mold easier). Serve (to adults) immediately.

STUNT DOUBLE CHOCOLATE MALT

Chocolate cravings are a real thing. Whether it's an emotional, hormonal, or physical need, I don't think it really matters. This delicious Stunt Double Chocolate Malt recipe helps me to "stand strong" when a chocolate craving hits (and tries to knock me down). It's so simple to make too. I use the leftover cold coffee from my morning pot to save a step. Bulletproof!

   1 cup cold coffee

   1 cup ice

   4 (1-gram) packets 0g net carbs sweetener

   1 small avocado, peeled, pitted, and mashed

   ¼ cup canned unsweetened, 12%–14% fat coconut milk

   1 tablespoon 100% cocoa powder

   ½ scoop low-carb chocolate protein powder

   ½ teaspoon pure vanilla extract

1 Put all ingredients in a blender. Pulse 30–60 seconds until desired consistency is reached, pausing to scrape the sides of the blender halfway through.

2 Pour malt into an extra-tall glass and enjoy immediately.

Pantry Staples

0g net carbs sweetener, pure vanilla extract

NET CARBS

5G

SERVES 1

PER SERVING	
CALORIES	378
FAT	27G
PROTEIN	17G
SODIUM	117MG
FIBER	11G
CARBOHYDRATES	17G
NET CARBS	5G
SUGAR	1G
SUGAR ALCOHOL	1G

TIME

PREP TIME:	5 MINUTES
COOK TIME:	0 MINUTES

TIPS & OPTIONS

Serve with a dollop of real whipped cream and a single raspberry. Perfection!

I set aside my ugly avocados to use in this recipe. You know what I'm talking about…the ones that become overripe or too *smushy* for their own good. They blend up perfectly in this drink.

BOOTLEG IRISH CREAM

Pantry Staples

0g net carbs sweetener, pure vanilla extract

NET CARBS

2G

SERVES 2

PER SERVING

CALORIES	316
FAT	21G
PROTEIN	1G
SODIUM	33MG
FIBER	0G
CARBOHYDRATES	3G
NET CARBS	2G
SUGAR	2G
SUGAR ALCOHOL	1G

TIME

PREP TIME:	5 MINUTES
COOK TIME:	0 MINUTES

TIPS & OPTIONS

This cocktail is best served chilled. Refrigerate remaining beverage until you're ready to enjoy.

Check out Walmart's Great Value Sugar Free Chocolate Flavored Syrup for this recipe. With 1g net carbs per 2-tablespoon serving, this brand gives you more bang for your buck when compared to the similar product made by Hershey's (1g net carbs per 1-tablespoon serving).

I like to drink a cocktail like Bootleg Irish Cream in the winter months when it's freezing outside. I serve the drink cold, but the creamy, smooth texture warms my soul (well, that and the whiskey!). Stoke up the fire and make a glass for you and your sweetheart. With a cup of Bootleg Irish Cream in each of your tumblers, it's sure going to get cozy tonight.

3 fluid ounces (2 shots) Irish whiskey

½ cup heavy whipping cream

2 tablespoons coffee

1 tablespoon sugar-free chocolate syrup

½ teaspoon 0g net carbs sweetener

⅛ teaspoon almond extract

¼ teaspoon pure vanilla extract

1 cup ice

1   In a blender, combine all ingredients except ice and pulse for a few seconds to mix.

2   Distribute even amounts of ice into two glass tumblers. Pour drink over ice and serve immediately.

MO MILK

Surprisingly, my entire family has made the transition to drinking solely almond milk. It just tastes better! We seem to always be running out. Desperation and thirst prompted me to figure out how to make this low-carb beverage at home. It was surprisingly uncomplicated. I wonder what's next for me....Will I be churning my own butter or growing my own vegetables? *Whoa, Nelly.* Homemade almond milk is one thing, but becoming a full-fledged pioneer woman sounds ridiculous.

> **2 cups unsalted, unroasted almonds**
>
> **6 cups water, plus more for soaking almonds**
>
> **¼ teaspoon salt**
>
> **1 tablespoon pure vanilla extract**

1   Add almonds to a medium bowl and cover with water. Cover with plastic wrap and soak overnight in the refrigerator (minimum 8 hours, preferably 12).

2   Drain and rinse almonds and add them to a blender along with 6 cups water and remaining ingredients. Blend on high 1–3 minutes until puréed. Stop and scrape the sides of the blender with a spatula as needed. (Depending on the size of your blender, you may elect to break up this step into batches.)

3   Cover a large pitcher with a four-ply layer of cheesecloth. Strain mixture through cheesecloth into the pitcher and discard pulp. If milk in the pitcher still contains almond residue, repeat straining process.

4   Store in the refrigerator until ready to serve. Serve chilled. Enjoy refrigerated within 4 days.

Pantry Staples

salt, pure vanilla extract

NET CARBS

1G

SERVES 8

PER SERVING

CALORIES	20
FAT	2G
PROTEIN	1G
SODIUM	72MG
FIBER	0G
CARBOHYDRATES	1G
NET CARBS	1G
SUGAR	0G
SUGAR ALCOHOL	0G

TIME

PREP TIME:	5 MINUTES, PLUS 8 HOURS (OR MORE) SOAKING TIME
COOK TIME:	0 MINUTES

TIPS & OPTIONS

Fans of the DLK PSL (Pumpkin Spice Latte) recipe in this chapter will be eager to try this fall-flavored trick. Sprinkle pumpkin pie spice into a cup of sweetened Mo Milk and warm in the microwave. *Delish.*

Want to try making chocolate almond milk? *This is so exciting....*Add ¼ cup 100% cocoa powder and 3 tablespoons 0g net carbs sweetener. It's not the Nestle Quik some of us grew up with, but it sure tastes low-carb *delicious*!

GLOW STICK MARGARITA

NET CARBS

0G

SERVES 2

PER SERVING

CALORIES	113
FAT	0G
PROTEIN	0G
SODIUM	11MG
FIBER	0G
CARBOHYDRATES	6G
NET CARBS	0G
SUGAR	0G
SUGAR ALCOHOL	6G

TIME

PREP TIME:	10 MINUTES
COOK TIME:	0 MINUTES

TIPS & OPTIONS »

Instead of enjoying a crushed-candy-rimmed drink, take the traditional route by using kosher salt or sea salt (as traditional as you can get while still using Jell-O to make a margarita!).

If a standard over-the-rocks margarita is desired, mix all ingredients well in a large pitcher and pour into salt-rimmed margarita glasses.

You can find the glow straws for this drink at several online retailers.

If the first sip of this Glow Stick Margarita doesn't make your eyes pop, then I don't know what will. The surprising rim of the glass and taste of the tart-flavored candy are just the beginning. Don't worry if you don't own a legit margarita glass; I don't either. Any clear wine glass will do. The important part is to see *the glow*.

3 sugar-free hard lemon candies

2 small limes

2 cups ice

1 cup unsweetened plain seltzer

3 fluid ounces (2 shots) tequila

1 teaspoon sugar-free lime gelatin mix

1 Place unwrapped candies into a small Ziploc bag. Finely crush with a rolling pin. Spread evenly on a small plate.

2 Cut one lime into quarters and use exposed flesh to wet the rims of two margarita glasses. Hold one glass upside down and press it into the crushed candy powder. Turn, if necessary, until entire rim is coated. Repeat with the second glass. Set aside.

3 Cut remaining lime in half. Holding the cut side up, squeeze 2 tablespoons juice into a blender. Slice lime into decorative wedges and hang one onto the edge of each glass.

4 Add remaining ingredients to the blender and pulse until desired consistency is achieved.

5 Pour evenly into candy-rimmed margarita glasses. Insert a glow drinking straw for stirring. Serve immediately.

NET CARBS
7G

SERVES 1

PER SERVING

CALORIES	252
FAT	17G
PROTEIN	13G
SODIUM	128MG
FIBER	2G
CARBOHYDRATES	9G
NET CARBS	7G
SUGAR	4G
SUGAR ALCOHOL	0G

TIME

PREP TIME:	5 MINUTES
COOK TIME:	0 MINUTES

TIPS & OPTIONS »

If a thicker smoothie is desired, use less water.

To prevent blender burnout, start by adding liquids first.

Top your smoothie with a sprinkle of sugar-free chocolate chips or a pinch of crushed sugar-free hard candy.

SNEAKY STRAWBERRY SMOOTHIE

I take my smoothies seriously—so much so that I bought a set of parfait spoons which I don't share (I don't want my spoons hiding in a dirty dishwasher!). I often need a spoon for smoothies (instead of a straw) because I like my drinks on the thicker side...*and then eat them like ice cream*. Good idea, right? This Sneaky Strawberry Smoothie is my go-to drink (slash dessert in disguise).

¾ cup ice

½ cup canned unsweetened, 12%–14% fat coconut milk

¾ cup water

½ scoop low-carb vanilla protein powder

½ cup frozen strawberries

¼ teaspoon pure vanilla extract

4 (1-gram) packets 0g net carbs sweetener

2 tablespoons unsweetened canned dairy whipped topping

1   In a blender, pulse all ingredients except whipped topping on high until desired consistency is achieved.

2   Pour into a tall glass and top with whipped topping. Serve immediately.

REBELLIOUS BLOODY MARY

Enjoy a Rebellious Bloody Mary for breakfast, lunch, or any time of day, really. *Who am I to say?* One of the many benefits of DIRTY, LAZY, KETO is that it's judgment-free. Only you get to say what goes! I, for one, am not willing to give up alcohol in order to lose weight. Call me a rebel if you want to, but I think a stiff drink is non-negotiable.

> **2 cups ice**
>
> **6 tablespoons plain vodka**
>
> **1 cup no-sugar-added tomato juice**
>
> **1 teaspoon 100% lemon juice**
>
> **¼ teaspoon hot sauce**
>
> **¼ teaspoon Worcestershire sauce**
>
> ✦ **¼ teaspoon salt**
>
> ✦ **⅛ teaspoon ground black pepper**

1   To a large shaker, add all ingredients except pepper and shake 30 seconds.

2   Strain evenly into two highball glasses. Evenly top with black pepper.

3   Serve immediately while still chilled.

Pantry Staples

salt, ground black pepper

NET CARBS

4G

SERVES 2

PER SERVING

CALORIES	117
FAT	0G
PROTEIN	1G
SODIUM	623MG
FIBER	1G
CARBOHYDRATES	5G
NET CARBS	4G
SUGAR	3G
SUGAR ALCOHOL	0G

TIME

PREP TIME:	5 MINUTES
COOK TIME:	0 MINUTES

TIPS & OPTIONS

Add a celery stick and a lemon wedge to each glass prior to serving.

A more elaborate garnish to try would be a decorative toothpick threaded with jumbo shrimp, fancy olives, and bacon. THAT look could become a DLK cover girl!

PEPPERMINT WHITE RUSSIAN

Fans of *The Big Lebowski* might remember Jeffrey "The Dude" constantly sipping this iconic drink. I, myself, can't imagine enjoying any more than one glass of this rich adult milkshake. With a bit of pink candy ringing the top, my Peppermint White Russian looks as good as it tastes. *Cheers!*

4 sugar-free hard peppermint candies

2 tablespoons water

1 cup ice

½ cup heavy whipping cream

¼ cup plain vodka

¼ cup espresso

2 (1-gram) packets 0g net carbs sweetener

1 Place unwrapped candy inside a Ziploc bag, seal the bag, and finely crush candy with a rolling pin. Spread contents onto a medium plate.

2 Pour water onto a small plate. Turn two old-fashioned glasses upside down and dip the rims first into water, then press them into candy mixture until rims are covered with candy.

3 Turn glasses right side up and evenly add ice.

4 Add remaining ingredients to a large shaker and seal.

5 Vigorously shake 5–10 seconds, then evenly pour drink over ice into glasses. Serve immediately.

Pantry Staples

0g net carbs sweetener

NET CARBS

2G

SERVES 2

PER SERVING	
CALORIES	291
FAT	21G
PROTEIN	1G
SODIUM	26MG
FIBER	0G
CARBOHYDRATES	12G
NET CARBS	2G
SUGAR	2G
SUGAR ALCOHOL	10G

TIME

PREP TIME:	10 MINUTES
COOK TIME:	0 MINUTES

TIPS & OPTIONS

Instead of heavy whipping cream, try substituting unsweetened vanilla almond milk (or any dairy alternative beverage). There are so many choices on the market these days! You can even use Mo Milk (see recipe in this chapter).

I stock up on sugar-free hard candy from my local dollar store for occasions like this.

NET CARBS

2G

SERVES 2

PER SERVING	
CALORIES	104
FAT	0G
PROTEIN	0G
SODIUM	1MG
FIBER	0G
CARBOHYDRATES	2G
NET CARBS	2G
SUGAR	0G
SUGAR ALCOHOL	0G

TIME

PREP TIME:	5 MINUTES
COOK TIME:	0 MINUTES

TIPS & OPTIONS

For a stronger mojito, cut back on the amount of diet soda added. The drink is clear, so a strong pour will not be obvious.

Rest assured that plain, unflavored hard alcohol (vodka, gin, rum, tequila, whiskey, brandy) all contain 0g net carbs per 1½-ounce serving. If that's not a DIRTY, LAZY, KETO miracle worth toasting to, then I don't know what is! *Cheers.*

TIPSY TIKI MOJITO

I want to let you in on a little secret: I have a makeshift tiki hut in my backyard! When the children are driving us bat-crazy, my husband and I escape to this tiny bit of paradise to sip a cocktail and enjoy a quiet conversation. Of course, no escape to paradise is complete without a summertime mojito in hand. We cherish every moment (and sip) of this unpretentious, sugar-free cocktail—that is, until the kids find us.

12 mint leaves

1 medium lime

3 fluid ounces (2 shots) plain white rum

2 cups crushed ice

10 ounces diet lemon-lime soda

1 Insert equal amounts of mint leaves into two tall glasses. Using the handle of a wooden spoon or spatula, "muddle" the leaves (bruise them a bit).

2 Cut lime in half. Holding the cut side up, squeeze equal amounts of juice into each glass. Cut lime into decorative wedges and set aside.

3 Add even amounts of rum, ice, and soda to the glasses and stir.

4 Garnish glasses with lime. Serve immediately.

ADDITIONAL RESOURCES

- For additional free resources, visit www.dirtylazyketo.com.
- Want direct support from Stephanie? Join the private, limited-enrollment, subscription-based Premium DIRTY, LAZY, KETO support group for women only, "DIRTY, LAZY, KETO Premium Support Group by Stephanie Laska." Join at http://bit.ly/SupporterDLK through the Premium link at https://www.facebook.com/becomesupporter/661359364046718/.
- Listen to the author directly on the free podcast *DIRTY, LAZY, Girl*, available wherever you listen to podcasts—links available at www.dirtylazyketo.com.
- Get involved in the DIRTY, LAZY, KETO community:
  - www.youtube.com/c/DIRTYLAZYKETOStephanieLaska
  - www.facebook.com/dirtylazyketo
  - www.facebook.com/groups/dirtylazyketo
  - www.instagram.com/dirtylazyketo
  - www.instagram.com/140lost
  - www.pinterest.com/dirtylazyketo
  - www.twitter.com/140lost

RECIPE RESOURCES

UNDERSTANDING RECIPE ICONS

Throughout the cookbook, you'll find special icons that highlight unique attributes of the recipes, such as:

 No Cook: Mix, fix, and enjoy! *Ultra lazy.*

 Less Mess: One pot—one bowl? *Minimal* dish-washing.

 I'm Hangry! Big-eater meals to *fill you up*!

 Picky Eaters? *He likes it! She likes it!* Crowd-pleasing favorites.

 Fancy Enough for Guests: *Ooh la la...* Looks impressive and tastes great!

 Vegetarian-"ish": *"Kinda"* meatless, but may still call for dairy and/or eggs.

CALCULATING RECIPE SERVING SIZES

The exact amount of a serving is clearly spelled out on nutrition labels but not in recipes. Why is that? There are too many variables involved with cooking to provide an exact amount. The size of eggs you use or the size of your pans directly affects how much food is made. But let's not overcomplicate this. In the spirit of Lazy Keto, put away your food scales and measuring cups when estimating what portion to serve yourself. Follow this simple calculation instead:

Divide the recipe quantity by the *yield* to determine the serving size.

If a lasagna serves eight people and has 9 grams of net carbs per serving, cut your lasagna into eight even pieces and enjoy. Each piece of lasagna is a single serving, meaning each piece will contain 9 grams of net carbs. Easy-peasy!

GLOSSARY

As a courtesy, I've included a glossary of how I am using common keto vocabulary. (Keep in mind that my definitions might be different from what you have heard before.)

KETO AND KETO FACTIONS

Dirty Keto

Dirty Keto is eating whatever foods you choose within your macro goals or limits (which are different for everyone). Unfortunately, there are a lot of misconceptions about Dirty Keto. Critics are horrified about including junk food or processed meats into one's diet. They assume we survive *solely* on hot dogs and sugar-free Red Bull! *That's just not true.* Instead, Dirty Keto empowers you with more flexible options about what to eat. There is no judgment or strict rules about your lifestyle. You might "eat clean" during the workweek but then live a little on the weekends. Foods aren't demonized either—artificial sweeteners and low-carb substitutes are fair game. Dirty Keto followers don't limit their food or beverage choices and might even be spotted drinking a Diet Coke (*oh, the horror!*).

DIRTY, LAZY, KETO

DIRTY, LAZY, KETO is not just a diet; it's a lifestyle. As a modern hybrid, it allows you to reap the benefits of losing weight, but without limitations of food choices or the obligation of counting every macro. We eat foods that are higher in fat, moderate in protein, and lower in carbs but allow for a little fun and flexibility. We are open to the idea of artificial sweeteners (Diet Coke or Splenda, for example) and include packaged foods (protein bars, low-carb tortillas) in our meals. Dirty *and* Lazy Keto followers count only net carbs. I am the superhero of this category! I even coined the term.

Keto

Keto is simply a shortened word for *ketogenic*.

Ketogenic diet

The ketogenic diet is a diet of foods high in fat, moderate in protein, and low in carbohydrates, with the goal of putting the body into ketosis.

Keto police

Keto police insist Strict Keto rules must be followed at all times! Though they don't wear a uniform, you can easily spot a member of the keto police by their social media posts that frequently ridicule others, arguing, "but THAT'S NOT KETO!" Keto police believe their purity and high standards make them superior; they constantly feel the need to educate and "correct" dissenting keto disciples.

Ketosis

Ketosis occurs when the body burns ketones from the liver as the main energy source (as opposed to using glucose, derived from carbs, as the energy source). Ketosis is often an indicator (but not a requirement) of weight loss.

Lazy Keto

Lazy Keto followers only count their net carb intake—not fat or protein intake. Lazy Keto does *not* mean unwilling to work hard for weight loss. This term refers to just one style of counting a single macro in keto—the net carb—not a relaxed lifestyle or lack of energy. Not tracking doesn't mean overconsumption, though! Common sense is *always* used.

Strict Keto

Strict Keto adheres to a rigid and closely monitored ketogenic diet consisting of no more than 20 grams of net carbohydrates per day. Followers insist on organic ingredients and avoid all processed foods. The keto prescription for weight loss never deviates: Calories are distributed to a perfect ratio of 75 percent fat, 20 percent protein, and 5 percent carbohydrates.

If you are not sure what keto camp you fall into, try taking the free, short quiz I created on my website at www.dirtylazyketo.com/quiz.

RELATED KETO TERMS

Calories

Calories are units of heat that food provides to the body. There are no "good" or "bad" calories. You've got to let this one go, people! A calorie is just an innocent unit of measurement, like a cup or a gallon. Our bodies *require* calories to survive. With DIRTY, LAZY, KETO, calories are not the focus (instead, net carbs are). The 1980s are over, my friends, and counting calories of low-fat foods is just as passé as leg warmers.

Carbohydrates/carbs

Carbohydrates, or carbs (for short), are sugars, starches, and fibers found in fruits, grains, vegetables, and milk products. Carbohydrates contain 4 calories per gram.

Chaffle

Chaffle started off as a portmanteau of *cheese waffles*, but the term has since evolved to include a variety of recipes made with a waffle maker.

Fat

Fat is the densest form of energy, providing 9 calories per gram. The most obvious example of fat is oil (olive, coconut, sesame, canola, vegetable, and so on). Less clear examples of fats are dairy foods, nuts, avocados, and oily fish. Some fats have a better reputation than others (think about how the media portrays eggs, mayonnaise, Alfredo sauce, or chicken skin). No matter the quality of the source, *fat is fat is fat.*

Fiber

Fiber is not digested by the body and is removed as waste. There are two types of fiber: soluble and insoluble. Fiber is a complex carbohydrate that does not raise blood sugar. *Fiber is your friend.*

Insoluble fiber

Insoluble fiber does *not* absorb water. Insoluble fiber moves through the intestine mostly intact, adding bulk to the stool and preventing constipation. Low-carb foods that contain notable amounts of insoluble fiber include blueberries, raspberries, strawberries, raw almonds, flaxseed, sesame seeds, walnuts, Brussels sprouts, cooked kale, and soybeans.

Keto flu

Keto flu is an avoidable set of symptoms (headache, lethargy, leg cramps) associated with dehydration, often experienced at the onset of the keto diet. Because the metabolic process of ketosis requires more water, increased hydration and electrolytes is required.

Macronutrients/macros

Macronutrients, or macros, come in three packages: *carbohydrates*, *protein*, and *fat*. All macronutrients are obtained through foods in the diet, as the body cannot produce them. Each macro fulfills vital roles for your health. All macros contain calories but at different densities. Carbohydrates and proteins have 4 calories per gram, and fat has 9 calories per gram.

Net carbs

Net carbs are the unit of measurement tracked in DIRTY, LAZY, KETO. On a nutrition label, net carbs are calculated by subtracting all fiber and sugar alcohol grams from the listed amount of carbohydrates. Total carbs, minus fiber, minus sugar alcohol, equals net carbs. Net carbs are the leftover carbs in this mathematical equation.

Protein

Protein has 4 calories per gram. Proteins take longer to digest because they are long-chain amino acids. Protein is largely found in meats, seafood, soy, dairy, eggs, legumes, and nuts.

Soluble fiber

Soluble fiber attracts water. When you eat foods high in soluble fiber, it turns to mush in your body. Soluble fiber absorbs water quickly and helps soften stool. It slows down digestion and helps you feel full. Examples of low-carb foods with notable amounts of soluble fiber include blackberries, strawberries, flaxseed, psyllium seed husks, artichokes, and soybeans.

Sugar alcohols

Sugar alcohols are reduced-calorie sweeteners. They do not contain alcohol! They are commonly used in sugar-free candy and low-carb desserts and are not digested by the body.

US/METRIC CONVERSION CHARTS

VOLUME CONVERSIONS

US VOLUME MEASURE	METRIC EQUIVALENT
⅛ teaspoon	0.5 milliliter
¼ teaspoon	1 milliliter
½ teaspoon	2 milliliters
1 teaspoon	5 milliliters
½ tablespoon	7 milliliters
1 tablespoon (3 teaspoons)	15 milliliters
2 tablespoons (1 fluid ounce)	30 milliliters
¼ cup (4 tablespoons)	60 milliliters
⅓ cup	90 milliliters
½ cup (4 fluid ounces)	125 milliliters
⅔ cup	160 milliliters
¾ cup (6 fluid ounces)	180 milliliters
1 cup (16 tablespoons)	250 milliliters
1 pint (2 cups)	500 milliliters
1 quart (4 cups)	1 liter (about)

WEIGHT CONVERSIONS

US VOLUME MEASURE	METRIC EQUIVALENT
½ ounce	15 grams
1 ounce	30 grams
2 ounces	60 grams
3 ounces	85 grams
¼ pound (4 ounces)	115 grams
½ pound (8 ounces)	225 grams
¾ pound (12 ounces)	340 grams
1 pound (16 ounces)	454 grams

OVEN TEMPERATURE CONVERSIONS

DEGREES FAHRENHEIT	DEGREES CELSIUS
200 degrees F	95 degrees C
250 degrees F	120 degrees C
275 degrees F	135 degrees C
300 degrees F	150 degrees C
325 degrees F	160 degrees C
350 degrees F	180 degrees C
375 degrees F	190 degrees C
400 degrees F	205 degrees C
425 degrees F	220 degrees C
450 degrees F	230 degrees C

BAKING PAN SIZES

AMERICAN	METRIC
8 × 1½ inch round baking pan	20 × 4 cm cake tin
9 × 1½ inch round baking pan	23 × 3.5 cm cake tin
11 × 7 × 1½ inch baking pan	28 × 18 × 4 cm baking tin
13 × 9 × 2 inch baking pan	30 × 20 × 5 cm baking tin
2 quart rectangular baking dish	30 × 20 × 3 cm baking tin
15 × 10 × 2 inch baking pan	30 × 25 × 2 cm baking tin (Swiss roll tin)
9 inch pie plate	22 × 4 or 23 × 4 cm pie plate
7 or 8 inch springform pan	18 or 20 cm springform or loose bottom cake tin
9 × 5 × 3 inch loaf pan	23 × 13 × 7 cm or 2 lb narrow loaf or pate tin
1½ quart casserole	1.5 liter casserole
2 quart casserole	2 liter casserole

INDEX

ABOUT THE AUTHORS

USA TODAY bestselling author and creator of DIRTY, LAZY, KETO, Stephanie Laska doesn't just talk the talk; she *walks the walk*. She is one of the few keto authors who has successfully lost half of her body weight (140 pounds!) and maintained that weight loss for eight years *and counting*.

Want the full story on how you, too, can lose weight for good? Check out the blockbuster *DIRTY, LAZY, KETO*: *Get Started Losing Weight While Breaking the Rules* (St. Martin's Essentials, 2020), the guidebook that started an international trend to help hundreds of thousands of fans lose weight in a revolutionary new way.

Expect humor, honesty, and inspiration from your DLK girlfriend, Stephanie Laska. Her mission is to help as many people as possible fight obesity *one carb at a time*! She fights back against the shame, blame, and judgment surrounding obesity with DIRTY, LAZY, KETO.

Stephanie's honest sass and fresh approach to the keto diet break all the traditional rules of dieting. You might have caught her cooking debut with Al Roker on NBC's *Today* show. Her story and image have been celebrated in articles or images shared by *Parade*, Fox News, *US News & World Report*, *New York Post*, *Reader's Digest*, *Women's Health*, *First for Women*, *Woman's World*, *Muscle & Fitness: Hers*, *Men's Journal*, *Keto for You*, runDisney, and *Costco Connection*. She has run a dozen marathons—most notably the New York City Marathon as a sponsored athlete from PowerBar. Not bad for a girl who ran her first mile (as in ever!) at close to age forty.

Alongside her coauthor and husband, William Laska, Stephanie has created more support tools: *The DIRTY, LAZY, KETO* *No Time to Cook Cookbook* (Simon & Schuster, 2021), *The DIRTY, LAZY, KETO* *Dirt Cheap Cookbook* (Simon & Schuster, 2020), *The DIRTY, LAZY, KETO* *Cookbook: Bend the Rules to Lose the*

Weight! (Simon & Schuster, 2020), and *DIRTY, LAZY, KETO* *Fast Food Guide: 10 Carbs or Less* (2018). Stephanie also hosts a free weekly podcast, *DIRTY, LAZY, Girl*, available for watching on the DIRTY, LAZY, KETO *YouTube* channel or for audio only on Apple Podcasts, Spotify, or wherever you listen to podcasts.

Stephanie and Bill reside in sunny California. When they aren't talking about their third child (DIRTY, LAZY, KETO), the Laskas enjoy running, traveling "on the cheap," and shopping at thrift stores.

IT'S THE KETO DIET FOR THE REST OF US!

BEND THE RULES TO LOSE THE WEIGHT!

THE **DIRTY, LAZY, KETO®** COOKBOOK

Topless Burgers, Birthday Cheesecake, Stuffed Party Shrooms— **100** Affordable Recipes, All Less Than 10g Net Carbs!

Stephanie Laska, MEd, and William Laska

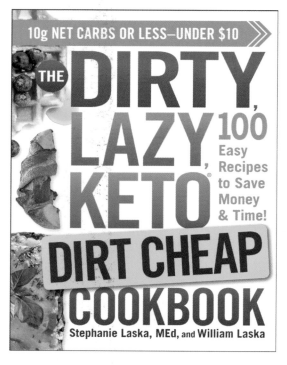

10g NET CARBS OR LESS—UNDER $10

THE **DIRTY, LAZY, KETO®** **DIRT CHEAP** COOKBOOK

100 Easy Recipes to Save Money & Time!

Stephanie Laska, MEd, and William Laska

QUICK-FIX MEALS WITH 10g NET CARBS OR LESS!

THE **DIRTY, LAZY, KETO®** *NO TIME TO COOK* COOKBOOK

100 Easy Recipes Ready in under 30 Minutes

Stephanie Laska, MEd, and William Laska

PICK UP OR DOWNLOAD YOUR COPIES TODAY!

adamsmedia
An Imprint of Simon & Schuster
A ViacomCBS COMPANY